IN THE FRONT COVER PHOTOGRAPH FROM LEFT TO RIGHT ARE:

ELROY GARDEN, LORNE MCCUISH, CARRIE-JANE GRAY, HAROLD MOFFAT, ALFRED NUNWEILER, JACK HEINRICH, JOSEPH TER HEIDE.

HAROLD MOFFAT

and

THE NORTHERN HARDWARE:

Prince George Icons

"If we don't have it; you don't need it."

VALERIE GILES PHD

Library and Archives Canada Cataloguing in Publication

Giles, Valerie M. E. (Valerie Mary Evelyn)
      Harold Moffat and the Northern Hardware : Prince George Icons / Valerie Giles.

Includes index.
ISBN-13: 978-0-9735422-3-3
ISBN-10: 0-9735422-3-3

      1. Moffat, Harold. 2. Prince George (B.C.)--Biography.
3. Prince George (B.C.)--History. I. Title.

FC3849.P7Z49 2006   971.1'8204092   C2006-906877-1

Design: PressForward
Index: Kathy Plett

c/o Valerie Giles, PhD
2676 Hollandia Drive
Prince George, B.C. V2N 4K9
Canada

Contents

"If we don't have it; you don't need it."

The Moffat Story
Introduction

This book is an undertaking about the life of Harold Alexander Moffat, the Northern Hardware & Furniture Co. Ltd. and Prince George. It is impossible to tell the story of any one – whether the person, the business or the city, without reference to the other two. So inextricably linked is the personal, corporate and civic life that each forms part of the other's history.

When I moved to Prince George in 1993, I was told by Paul St. Pierre (the celebrated author of newspaper commentary, plays and books about life in this region) that I would never understand the heart and soul of Prince George until I met and talked with Harold Moffat. Paul is an astute observer and student of human nature and as my friend of four decades, I tend to take notice of what he has to say and generally heed his advice.

During my first month here, I spent lunch hours exploring the downtown. One day, I walked into the hardware store and inquired if that was the right place to find Harold Moffat. A bright young individual pointed him out across the store. I thanked the employee, and explained that I would come back when I had time to introduce myself. In the time it took to say that, Harold Moffat was at my side asking about my interest and why he was being pointed at! I had to admit I'd been sent to find him. He responded cordially and said, "I'll talk to you.

Come back at 4:00." I did. For an hour and a half he regaled me with stories about the early years in Prince George, the way the business was run during the Depression and war years, and some of the unique events that swirled around the life of the business he inherited from his father.

In the days following, those stories began to intrigue me more. I decided to approach him about doing interviews to record his experience. Taking into account the longtime operation of the business, nearly a quarter century service on the school board and almost a decade as Mayor, Harold Moffat's life constitutes a fairly well-rounded history of the city of Prince George. I was excited at the chance to record this history so it could be shared with others.

I thought it might be a selling point to suggest to him that we could record audio tapes and deposit them in the Prince George Library. Not knowing then of his indifference to that particular building and institution, it was a naive suggestion which did not move him. He declined and feigned a total lack of interest. For two and a half years he avoided my entreaties to reconsider. In the fall of 1995, he changed his mind. That September 24 marked Harold Moffat's 80th birthday, and that summer the Moffats had gathered to celebrate their 105-year family history. Those events helped firm up the notion that there was a story to tell and, finally, he agreed. My persistence was rewarded and I had demonstrated my genuine interest in the project. We could begin.

The pages of this book are crafted from hours of interviews with Harold Moffat and those who know him and from the extensive records extant in the library, city archives, school board and the Northern Hardware. It is my fond wish that I will have told the story well, and that people who don't live in Prince George will gain an appreciation for the tenacity that residents demonstrate in coping with the challenges of a winter climate, encounters with wild animals, and geographic isolation from larger cities.

For anyone wondering why early pioneers or recent arrivals would choose to come here and live with snow and ice for five months of the year on the fringes of wilderness, some explanations can be found in the pages following. Try a visit here in the dead of winter. Choose a night with a full moon and go for a walk. Watch the diamond-dusted snow glisten in the moonlight, hear the crunch of snow under your feet and let the cold envelop and clear your head. You may find the experience invigorating, and since development of the city has not affected the snow and cold, it is one way you can connect with and share the adventure of those who travelled and lived here before you. This challenging experience may well turn out to be a beautiful, momentous occasion which will add to your personal lore and store of memories.

Most of all, I hope I have captured the essence of a unique person and a family business which has grown along with the City of Prince George from its earliest years.

– Valerie Giles

CHAPTER I

The Patriarch—Harry Henry Moffat
The First Moffat in the Cariboo

Harry Henry Moffat (1853 - 1947)
"Patriarch Passes In Quesnel"[1]

Harold Moffat's grandfather, Harry Henry Moffat, died on Saturday March 15, 1947 at the age of 94. His funeral, reported under this front page headline, was conducted by Reverend J.H. Hobbins the following Tuesday afternoon in Quesnel's St. Andrew's United Church. In attendance were "cowboys from the far-off Chilcotin, Indians, Chinese, miners, ranchers and businessmen from throughout the Cariboo."[2] Their presence signalled the respect and affection all those people held for him. The church was packed to the doors and an estimated 200 more stood on the street outside. A resolutely religious man, with a reputation for strength of character and fair-mindedness, his life was filled with interesting work, a large family, and many friends. That day, they bade him farewell, reflecting on the kind of man he was and how his life had been lived. Also represented was the Order of Masons. They conducted a graveside ritual for their longtime member.

---

[1] Prince George Citizen, 20 March 1947, p. 1
[2] Ibid.

As a young man of 21, Harry Moffat left his home in Pembroke, Ontario where he had been born on Christmas Day, 1853. Raised by Scottish immigrant parents[3] who instilled in him a sense of purpose and independence, that background served him well for the adventures to come. He travelled overland to San Francisco, sailing on the paddle wheel steamer *Pacific* back to Canada, landing at Victoria on May 24, 1875.

Crossing to the mainland, he sought work at the Survey Headquarters in Kamloops. He got hired to join one of the crews which set out to establish the most feasible route for the Canadian Pacific Railway through the Rocky Mountains.

An account reported many decades later described the work as spread over a vast territory: "The party first traversed the country east from Bute Inlet in the central interior of British Columbia ... his survey party worked up the North Thompson River from Kamloops to Tete Jaune Cache, thence down the Fraser River to Giscome Portage. In the fall of 1876, the survey party went down the Fraser from Giscome Portage to Quesnel and there disbanded."[4]

The local Moffat family consequently traces its origins in the central region of British

---

[3] The Moffat clan hails from Dumfriesshire in Southern Scotland where family history dates back to the late 1100s. The clan motto is *Spero Meliora* – "I hope for better things."
[4] *Prince George Citizen*, 29 August 1940, p. 2.

Columbia to the arrival in Quesnel of Harry Henry Moffat in 1876.

Literally, he was a trail blazer, for not only were some of his accomplishments firsts for this region, he helped open up remote territory by working on the survey crews and becoming familiar with the lay of the land and the opportunities at hand.

One example is that his attraction to placer mining eventually led into operation of a freighting business. Harry Moffat became a partner in the "Bank of England" claim at Williams Creek, which proved to be a rich one, and afterwards had an interest in the "Big Bonanaza" claim at Wingdam and in another property on Antler Creek.[5]

For a time, he drove the 98-mile stage route between 134 Mile House and Barkerville, and also between Ashcroft and Quesnel. He was considered an expert rangeman and was a man of extraordinary energy. It was his habit during winter to leave the horse and sleigh at Stanley and pack the mail on his back by snowshoe into Barkerville – a distance of fourteen miles.

Being energetic and wanting to settle, he pre-empted 320 acres of land and began clearing for a homestead near Alexandria. Realizing that miners needed reliable delivery of supplies, Harry investigated the possibility of providing freighting service on the Cariboo Road. He brought one of the first horse teams over the

---

[5] Ibid., p. 1.

road and thus began his own transportation business. His means of conveyance for goods and equipment departed from the more common one of the day, which was using bull teams. While he carried on with his freighting business, he hired Chinese labourers to accomplish the farm work.[6] When motor-driven conveyance replaced horses, the B.C. Express used a Winton Six vehicle, one of which was photographed at the Moffat Ranch in 1912.[7]

In 1885, he gave up the stage route but continued freighting and started turning his attention to his homestead. Eventually he built a large home and developed a fine ranch. In a spirit of patriotism, Harry named the ranch for the Marquess of Lansdowne, who had been named Governor General of Canada two years earlier in 1883. Harry operated a successful venture at Lansdowne with a combination of ranching and farming.

On August 25, 1890 he married Jennie (Jane Roddy) who was visiting from Ayrshire, Scotland. The couple's first son, Alexander Bohannon Moffat was born June 16, 1891, and eight other children (Roddy, Henry, Frances, Agnes, Aveline, May, Jack and Jim) came after that. All were born at Lansdowne except the last two sons whose births took place at the new Quesnel hospital. A.B. Moffat's first son was Harold Alexander Moffat, born September 24,

---

[6] *Quesnel Cariboo Observer*, 7 August 1985, 12.
[7] Archives, District Resource Centre, School District No. 57, Prince George.

1915, which is how the subject of this volume came to be.

The Moffats' home became a stopping place for the B.C. Express Stage Lines (known as the BX), teamsters and other travellers which meant a continuous stream of "guests" came and went from the home. A Chinese cook was hired to help Jennie prepare the meals. Travellers had breakfast served after the thirty-eight mile trip from Quesnel which took four hours over mud and gravel roads. Jennie also operated the community's post office from a wicket installed near the home's entrance and also provided a modest general store. Although her life was busy, she spent a lot of it alone while Harry travelled the distances in his freighting business. In the farm journals, she recorded where he went and all the visitors who came by.

Once, her husband's imminent return was reported by the stage driver who told her that Moffat was going to drop in and visit the ranch. There were cold days when she recorded "it is a snorter today blowing and drifting" and exasperating times as the notation "everything going to blazes backwards" reveals.[8] When her children reached school age, she and the children moved into their house in Quesnel, leaving hired help to operate the farm, and

---

[8] OAPO, Branch #77, Quesnel. *A Tribute to the Past: Quesnel & Area 1808-1928* (Quesnel: Spartan Printing), 74-75.

giving her some respite from all the activity of that busy life.[9]

During the first decade and a half of this century, the Conservatives (led by Richard McBride) kept winning elections and the right to form the provincial government. Perhaps the zenith of that power was realized in the 1909 election which Premier McBride called after a dispute with Ottawa.

McBride crafted his political campaign around the issue of railroads; specifically of building a third transcontinental railroad. He travelled the province with the message about all the advantages a railway would bring in attracting more population, expanding mercantile markets and boosting real estate values. He envisioned railway lines that would link the Yellowhead Pass and Vancouver; Victoria and Barkley Sound; and Midway and Nicola.[10] Ribbons of steel would connect the hinterland to commercial centres for the benefit of all.

Diverting attention from the complicated contractual arrangements behind the scenes, the public eagerly took up support of the Premier's message of coming prosperity. His government was not only returned, but managed

---

[9] The other home was at the corner of McLean Street and Barlow Avenue in Quesnel.

[10] Martin Robin, *The Company Province 1871-1933* (Toronto: McClelland and Stewart 1972), 109-110.

to win all but four seats.[11]   Clearly, public support was on the side of expanding and improving transportation links within the province.[12]

All governments rely on loyal supporters to get elected into office in the first instance, and afterwards need them to remain in power and accomplish the party's political agendas.   The Conservative government had such a backer in Harry Moffat and his loyalty was rewarded with an appointment as district road superintendent in 1910.

Travel then by horse-drawn conveyance during winter months was a challenge, particularly if the horses went off the narrow (just the width of a team) packed-down trail. Harry devised a contraption that would flatten the surface to create an eight foot path, which was essentially the width of the road. He used a large roller, pulled by four horses, to flatten the snow "as hard and as level as a paved city street."   The accomplishment was lauded in a newspaper account which declared "Snow Roller A Decided Success."[13]

In 1908, Harry's second son, Roddy Roy, joined him in the freighting business.   People

---

[11] S.W. Jackman, *Portraits of the Premiers: An Informal History of British Columbia* (Sidney: Gray's Publishing Ltd. 1969), 161.
[12] *Cariboo Observer*, 18 September 1909, 1. Formal legal notice given of the intention to apply to the Legislative Assembly for an act to incorporate a company "to construct, equip, maintain and operate a line or lines of railway" that would link together remote communities throughout British Columbia.
[13] *Cariboo Observer*, 27 January 1912.

living at Barkerville were steady customers for the produce raised at Lansdowne Farm. Loaded with vegetables and meat, they headed out to Barkerville. In good weather, they took a week to complete the round trip. This proved a successful introduction because within a year, he was able to begin his own freighting venture.

Eventually, Roddy came back to the farm and ran it with his next younger brother, Henry. With the outbreak of the First World War in 1914, Henry left for overseas service. Upon his return in 1918, his father handed Lansdowne Farm over to him. Subsequently, Harry began developing another ranch, a little closer to Quesnel at Sister Creek, and ultimately retired in Quesnel.

Retirement came in June of 1927 when he was 74. The occasion was momentous enough to warrant a newspaper headline and a front page account indicating that his herd was for sale:

> Harry Moffat, father of Alderman A.B. Moffat, has decided that he is too old to continue in the dairy business at Alexandria and on Saturday he arrived in this city with his entire herd of 26 Ayrshire stock.
>
> Each of the animals is certified under the T.B. test. The herd is headed by a bull sired by Peter Pan, out of Lady Laura, the champion cow of B.C. in her

time. The animals may be seen at the Thompson ranch, across the river.[14]

HARRY MOFFAT RIDING PETE

Memories of Grandpa Harry Henry Moffat were recalled by Helen Moffat years later.

---

[14] "Harry Moffat Decides To Retire From Dairy Business In Alexandria," Prince George Citizen, 30 June 1927, front page.

On the occasion of the grandparents' fiftieth wedding anniversary in 1940, Harold and Helen and their firstborn, Ted, travelled to Quesnel for the celebration. Helen retains vivid memories about that trip:

Yes, we were there. I took Teddy and he would have been one year old. He was in the car and I can remember holding him on my knees and I took off his shoes. He had little boots. It was important to have your children in good shoes so they could learn to walk. But who wants to be trodden over on your legs with these little boots? So I took them off. I remember Alex saying 'Doesn't that kid have any shoes?' Harold had to explain that we'd taken them off for the ride down. Alex was a little embarrassed because he thought it looked bad for his grandchild not to have any shoes on his feet!

I don't remember too much about it because I was likely outside a lot with Ted. Harold's Dad had a movie camera. We always took lots of pictures. Unfortunately, the pictures were gorgeous, all in colour, great bouquets of gladiola, but there must have been a little cog that slipped out so the film jumped all the time. You just barely get the picture. We finally got one still made out of the tape.[15]

Over the years, Helen made many visits to Quesnel to visit friends Mary and Lloyd Harper who was in the sheet metal business there:

I used to take Ted (before I had Marilyn and Valerie). I used to go down and spend a weekend. And then I'd go to visit Granny Moffat. She had her house and Grandpa had his. Grandpa was a very strong Mason and Presbyterian and she was a Roman Catholic. As a couple, they would get into arguments.

Visits among family members kept up over the years, with Grandpa Moffat travelling to Prince George to visit his son, Alex.

Helen Moffat recalls:

He used to sit down in the store. He would be well into his eighties or maybe into his nineties by then, a very old man. Harold would bring him up to our house. He'd have dinner with us at noon. I can remember I had Ted in his own crib in his own bedroom. Grandpa said, "You should move him into your own bedroom, he's too far away at night. Something may happen to him." He was probably a year old. But, I said, "Okay, Grandpa, I will."

---

[15] Interview with Helen Moffat, 23 July 1997.

But by that time Ted was quite happy in his little crib in his own room. There was only one wall between us and I could hear him. Houses weren't soundproof like they are now. However, it was the common practice then that children were kept in the same bedroom with their parents until they went to school.[16]

In personality, Grandpa Moffat was kindly, and never stern. In Helen's own words, he is remembered very fondly:

He was a deeply religious man. I can remember him coming to visit me, stopping to visit me when I was at Mary Harper's – just stopping at the door – and he recited to me that passage which begins "May the Lord lift up his countenance upon thee. . ." and he gave it all off by heart word for word as we stood there on the porch.[17] That was the kind of man he was. A dear, a really dear man.

But, I think probably ruthless in some ways when he was younger. They had to have a certain amount of that to stand the rigours. Imagine going all the way by horseback to Barkerville to go to a Masonic meeting in the dead of winter! You had to be a little rough.

---

[16] Ibid.
[17] Scripture from Numbers 6:24.

He also had a soft side. His children meant a lot to him, and Granny Moffat the same. She was a character. I often think about it. I think originally she was a Boston girl. Can you imagine landing up out on a ranch? All those places were like a road house. People arrived and you bedded them down and you fed them. She would have to do all the cooking.

Harry, well, men never did any cooking or that sort of thing in those days. So Harry Moffat would sit and smoke his pipe and talk over the affairs of the day, see to the travellers, and then there were all these children. She had a baby every year.[18] And they were all great people.

Because Harold and I knew that family better than Harold's sisters and brothers, we got to know all of Harold's aunts and uncles. They all became very proud of Harold. Many of them were still around when Harold became Mayor and were aware of many of his achievements – like becoming Citizen of the Year – and some of the other accolades. They shared them with him and were very proud and made sure they wrote a little note. Especially after

---

[18] Jennie Moffat had her first baby when she was 22 and the last baby when she was 38. She spent almost her entire adult life pregnant.

Harold's Dad died, because a lot of things he did were after that.[19]

---

[19] Interview with Helen Moffat, 23 July 1997.

CHAPTER II

The Father – Alexander Bohannon Moffat
Establishing in Prince George
Founder of The Northern Hardware

Alexander Bohannon Moffat
(16 June 1891 - 24 January 1963)

Born June 16, 1891 at his parents' Lansdowne Ranch[20] near Alexandria, Alexander Bohannon Moffat was named for the town of his birth and for his father's friend[21]. Having become a stopping point for the stage, arriving passengers were greeted with the news that a baby boy had been born. That incident was recalled during John A. Fraser's speech to the regular Friday Rotary Club luncheon years later in 1947. "You were that baby," John Fraser told A.B. Moffat. He went on to describe how the passengers all went in to see him.[22]

During his remarkable 72-year life, he saw and participated in some dramatic changes in

---

[20] Harry Henry Moffat named his ranch after Lansdowne Farms in Pembroke, Ontario where he had lived before moving to British Columbia.

[21] Harry Moffat admitted that he hoped naming his son Bohannon would create a bond with his wealthy friend who had no children. He hoped that the gesture might create a future inheritance from Bohannon.

[22] Speech by John A. Fraser to the Rotary Luncheon 14 February 1947, and reported in "Babies Big News In Earlier Days," Prince George Citizen 20 February 1947, front page.

commerce, in the social and political organization of the region and in the growth of Prince George.

Alex grew up within a mixed marriage: a Presbyterian father and a Roman Catholic mother, who respected each other's faith and came to an agreement about raising their family regarding religion. When firstborn Alex was still a baby, his parents decided that all their boys would be Protestants and all their girls Catholics. Harold recalled, "My father called himself a 'near Catholic' and always had a soft spot in his heart for the priests and clergy."[23]

Spending his childhood on the farm, and moving into Quesnel with his mother and siblings to attend school, Alex encountered a recently-arrived Englishman, John A. Fraser, as his first teacher.[24] The teacher changed careers and operated a general store in Quesnel. While a schoolboy, the former teacher hired Alex to sweep the store and keep the fires stoked. After John Fraser became elected a Member of Parliament, he was required to leave his store for long periods of time. Returning from one long trip, he paid Alex several months' wages, and happened to inquire what he was going to do with the money. "Buy a pair of chaps from Eaton's" was the reply. John Fraser pointed to

[23] Notes penned by Harold Moffat for a booklet *The Moffat Family 1890-1995*, prepared for distribution to family members at the 1995 reunion., the year of the 120th anniversary of founding Lansdowne Farm, p. 23.

[24] The teacher's son grew up to become the Hon. Alex Fraser, Minister of Highways for British Columbia.

the chaps hanging in his own store and proceeded to fire the young Moffat boy. That was the day Alex was taught a lesson about loyalty.

In due time Alex reached the age where he needed to attend high school. That meant moving to Vancouver, and once there the dutiful son wrote to his father providing an account of the cold ride by saddle horse through minus 38 degree weather, an explanation for his decision to go to business college rather than high school, an accounting to the penny of how he'd spent the $60.00 his father had given him and, like all students, a request for more funds!

During the long ride to Vancouver, the freezing January temperature and blowing wind were so extreme that Alex had to dismount and walk behind the horse to keep warm. There were times along the route that he actually tied himself to his horse's tail to prevent himself from stopping.[25]

When considering his training options, Alex kept in mind that the government hired gold commissioners and telegraph operators. He respectfully explained in the letter that unlike his friend Alfred Brown, he was not going to high school because he had gone there and discovered that the course of studies included subjects like French, Greek, Latin and Algebra "and a lot of stuff that takes five or six years to learn."

---

[25] Harold Moffat, *The Moffat Family 1890-1995, p. 23.*

The expectation had been that he would spend perhaps three to six months getting schooling and then would come back. He decided that business college was his most practical option, and offered a curriculum of English, Penmanship, Arithmetic, Rapid Calculation, Bookkeeping and Correspondence. The college also offered telegraphy and typewriting, which Alex offered to take in addition if his father advised it.

He commented that his impression of Vancouver was that it was a busy city and everyone seemed to be well-off. Writing home just five days after his arrival, he admitted "I do not like the city at all and feel sometimes like coming right back." After requesting another $73.00 for tuition, board and books, Alex appended his detailed accounting of the money spent to date and signed "Your affectionate son, Alex."[26]

The business training proved a good choice, for a decade later, Alex formed a partnership with Frank D. Whitmore and purchased the assets of Northern Lumber, which evolved into the Northern Hardware and Furniture Company Limited.

---

[26] See full text of the letter on pages 19 - 22. It is enough to make any parent wistful!

I

683 Hamilton St.
Vancouver, B.C.
Jan 15, 1907.

Dear Father,—

I arrived here
Sunday Jan. 10th all O. K.,
I had a cold ride on the
way down, 38 below one day.
& never less than eight, I hope
you are all well & not froze
for it must be still cold
up there for it is 8 above here
now, & this is considered very
cold here. This is a very busy
City every body seems to be well-off.
That Sixty Dollars did not
last me long. enclosed you will
find a list of things purchased
& how it went, I had quite a
time getting a boarding house,

HANDWRITTEN LETTER AND EXPENSES LIST, PAGE 1

II

Alfred Brown is paying 25.ºº for
his board but I got mine for
$23.ºº I am not staying with
him as I am not going to the
High School for this reason.
I went one day to see what
it is like, you get French,
Greek, Latin, Algebra, and a
lot of stuff that takes 5 or
six years to learn and that in
3 or 6 mos. you would hardly
get started in so I have taken
a course in a Business College
at $15 a mo. or $40.ºº for 3 mos.
with books about $10.ºº thats
$50.ºº besides my board & clothes
of course I have got enough
clothes now, but it is going to

HANDWRITTEN LETTER AND EXPENSES LIST, PAGE 2

cost terrific. I left the mare
in W. Hustons charge but he
says it will cost $5.00 a mo. to
keep her & that is awfully steep.
The 2 in. Bob sleighs I could not
get in Ashcroft for they had not
any in stock. now if I am going
to stop here and go ~~the~~ that buisness
college for 3 months I should
~~get~~ take advantage of the $40.00
for 3 mo. & not pay them $15.00 a
mo. I made arrangements for them
to wait until I got the money, as
it is in advance there. now if this
is too steep I can just take a mo.
course & come ~~Home~~ with my
books & study there. I do not
like the City at all & feel

IV—

Remit as soon as possible as they are giving me Credit at the College.

some-time like coming right back. I am tak'ing English, Penmanship, Arithmetic, Rapid Calculation, Book-keeping & Correspondence & can take teligraphy & typewriting if you advise it. I stayed over night at the 150 M. H. going down) & Mr. Cunliff told me that he was thinking of getting me there for the summer, but when I get back the first thing is to get up to Mud River with Little & take up a cattle Ranch.

Well no more this time, write often & remit by money-order or by sight-draft.

your affectionate
son Alf.

Address, 683 Hamilton St.
van.

Owing College for Purse 40.00
next mo. board 23.00
Books $63.00
10.00
remit. $73.00

1 suit case 2.75
4 fare Ash. to Van. 8.15
2 meals on way 1.00
1 room at Hotel 2 days 2.00
meals at resturant 2 days 1.25
1 comb 25
stamps, envelopes, ink, paper 50
1 suit clothes Jan. Sale. 9.75
3 shirts 2.15
2 collars & tie 75
1 pr. braces & cap .75
2 suits under wear 2.00
1 watch 2.50
handkerchiefs 25 oranges 25 50
2 tickets to th 25
1 mo. board 23.00
$57.55

Bal. left $3.00

HANDWRITTEN LETTER AND EXPENSES LIST, PAGE 5

As a young man, Alex began work in the freighting business – driving stage coaches on the routes south from the Alexandria area and between Ashcroft and Barkerville. It was during that time when he became interested in and involved with the Masons. He spent five years passing through the various orders in the Masonic hierarchy.

A.B. Moffat arrived in South Fort George in 1912. He boarded at the Northern Hotel. His first job here was working at sawing wood for 25 cents a cord. The next job was as time keeper for Public Works.

He married Emma Cameron in 1914 and set up a family home in South Fort George.

Harold Alexander Moffat was born September 24th, 1915 in the family home which was later brought downtown to 8th Avenue. He was the first and only child of Alexander Bohannan Moffat and Emma Cameron. The next year, his parents adopted a little girl whose mother had died in childbirth. Her name was Alice Trainer, who was then renamed Alice Cameron Moffat for her adoptive mother.

When Harold was just fifteen months old, his mother wrote to her sister, Evelyn, to thank her for the gifts received for Christmas of 1916. She provides the earliest available description of what her son was like:

> I tell you we have some boy. He is a bit lazy as he will not walk, but I don't much blame him, he can creep so fast.

If I stand him in the middle of the floor and tell him to walk, he will, but does not want to go on his own.

He can say quite a number of words. The first he ever said was "Who's that," – he can say it as plain as we can. He started that about four months ago[27] and has never forgotten it.[28]

Life changed dramatically for A.B. in 1916 with the employment he found next. He joined on as part of a survey crew working west of Prince George. They were scouting out the path to create a shorter travel distance from Vanderhoof to Fraser Lake. Once he became familiar with the area, A.B. pre-empted land in Fraser Lake. Later on, that decision proved valuable when he was able to leverage the land for his next business venture.

Emma died in childbirth. With that sad event, a housekeeper, Mrs. Henry, came to live in and raise Harold and Alice. She had been the mother of a large family, and was elderly by the time she came to work for the Moffat family. She lived at her own home, but came over to spend days with the Moffat children. Harold remembers her as a very kind lady.

---

[27] Documentary evidence that Harold Moffat began speaking when he was only eleven months old.

[28] Letter dated 8 January 1917 at South Fort George, written by Emma Moffat to her sister, Evelyn.

Eventually, A.B. Moffat, remarried. His second wife was Florence Avis Horwood, who retired from teaching to marry. She came from a religious Methodist-based family.

MOFFAT FAMILY HOME

Following their wedding in Vancouver, the couple returned here, travelling back through the province by car and stopping at the Alexandria Ranch to pick up Harold. A new family home was purchased at the corner of Hammond and Moffat in Central Fort George. Still standing, it was designed as a spacious log home with a large verandah and a roof opening to accommodate a row of eleven windows to let light into the upstairs.

During her marriage, Florence bore six sons (Keith, Lorne, Donn, Earl, John, and Gilbert) and two daughters (Betty and Joyce). There was not much discipline, she wasn't harsh – but it was also difficult for her to oversee that many children. She tried to make the children stay quiet. Harold and sister Alice took piano lessons. It was a lively home, and although Florence didn't approve of liquor, Harold remembers that whenever his stepmother was worn down, Dr. Ewert prescribed Guinness stout as the cure for her flagging energy level. Occasionally, there was help hired with the housework. A.B. Moffat eventually hired a Chinese cook who lived in a cabin beside the house.

In the Depression years, Harold recalled that his stepmother (he called her "Mother") expressed surprise at how all the children survived and nobody ended up in the hospital. By modern standards of nutrition, this was remarkable because they lived on starch. Potatoes were always available because they were commonly brought in by customers to use as barter for hardware.

In those years, Harold spent a great deal of time packing and cutting wood for the garage, the chicken house and the home. The house was always chilly, there was just no warmth apart from that generated by a kitchen stove and heater. The biggest fireplace in Prince George was the one in their living room, and that is where the family gathered to keep warm.

The home had a big round dining table. At one point, the stepmother's sister came up to

Prince George and stayed with them. She bought a ladies' wear business and continued to live with them.

There was a piano in the living room. Harold recalled, "Mother played a bit, but more often guests would come and play it. Father worked almost every evening at the store. There was a lot of work to do in marking prices on goods."

Introduction to store work came when Harold was 12 years old. He was set to the task of stocktaking which had to be done at night. He watched a man named Matheson assist Mr. Whitmore. Mr. Matheson wrote down how many of each item and at what price. Inventory at the store during the 1990s was still done the same way. Harold said then "We've been doing stocktaking like this for 68 years. We aren't computerized, we do it 'backwards,' not the modern way!"

In the evenings, his father would bring Harold back to the store. All the children and grandchildren, once they reached twelve, would be brought to the store to help with the inventory count. Everyone got a start in the family business the same way. Another rite of passage in becoming twelve was when Harold taught all his grandchildren to drive the car on the farm. There were twin grandsons who at 10 expressed interest in being granted the work and driving privileges.

Other than for recognition of holidays, the store has never been closed except for one day, and that was when his father bought out his partner. There had to be a break in business for accounting purposes, and that was accomplished by closing the store.

Maintaining the store was also done by the family members. Basement areas and warehouses were kept up during off times or on Sundays.

Father Alex always came home for supper in the evening. But, he had to go back to the store to check the air compressor. The store kept one so the Northern could supply free air. Within a few months of opening the store, The Northern Hardware Co. ran this advertisement in the newspaper:

CAR OWNERS
We have just installed a
Free Air Station

in connection with our auto accessory line and wish every car owner to take advantage of it, whether you believe in buying your accessories from us or not. This station is open both day and night.

We are agents for the Maltese Cross, Firestone and Partridge Tubes and Casings, with a stock on hand at all times.

Look over our stock of Accessories, including our line of Auto Enamels.[29]

Harold recalls that his father was proud of that free air station. It was a good service, and there were some regulars who availed themselves of it. Suddenly, the device began registering almost empty every morning. A.B. Moffat worked for hours to try to find where the system had a leak, including digging up part of the sidewalk. The mystery was solved, finally, when another customer informed him that Scotty Buchanan was one who was always there every morning using the compressor. He would let all the air out of his car tires and then refill them. He believed it did his vehicle good to put in "fresh air" every day!!!

Harold learned from his father the belief that the customer came first. As a personality, he remembers him as outgoing, and as someone who always acknowledged people. "He was a real gentleman."

Harold's memories of his father are associated with a strong positive attitude and a solid commitment to promoting community welfare. In that capacity, he provided leadership and support for Knox United Church, the Chamber of Commerce, the School Board, and a variety of sports clubs. At the beginning of 1940, he donated a carpet to the Library. That was a rather generous contribution at a time

---

[29] Advertisement published in the Prince George Citizen, 30 April 1919, p. 6.

when the city's grant to the provincially-funded library was just $10.00 that year[30].

As a community event, it would be difficult to conjure up something more characteristically Prince George than "The Great Barrel Race" and A.B. Moffat was responsible for that inspiration, thought up shortly after the Prince George Rotary Club formed in 1943.

For Rotary's first fundraising event, club director A.B. Moffat chaired the publicity campaign to generate interest in guessing how long it would take a barrel to float down the Fraser River from the bridge at Dome Creek, through the canyon, and arrive at the steel bridge in Prince George.

To promote interest in making bets on the number of hours it would take to run the 145 mile route, A.B. Moffat used space in his store's front window. A large map showed the route, river currents and main towns along the way.

Alongside the map in The Northern's window was the red-striped barrel and a poster promoting the July 3 event. Launched under cover of darkness at 3:00 a.m., the first barrel got caught in a log boom and a second one had to be launched the next day at 3:00 a.m. This time, the barrel made it through in 47 hours 59.5 minutes. The top prize of $300 was shared among six people who estimated 48 hours. The

---

[30] "At the Library," Prince George Citizen, 25 January 1940, p. 5.

event was declared an outstanding success, raising $1,000 for charity.

Always imaginative and homey, the Christmas windows at The Northern have delighted generations of customers. A.B. Moffat started that, and Harold carried on the tradition. Some years, an artist would be engaged to paint Christmas scenes "backwards" on the glass so they'd be enjoyed by people walking by on the sidewalk.

The Northern's Canoe Races were held annually up until the last year, 1984. Another fun event was the high interest taken in betting odds on how long it would take for an ice-encased lawnmower to melt – prominently displayed outside the store's entrance.

A.B. Moffat got behind community events sponsored by other organizations. For years up until recent decades, The Northern had a float in the Elks' annual May Day parade. A staff member would volunteer to put the float together...from coming up with the idea to execution of the parade entry.

An example of A.B. Moffat's social activisim was prominent in March of 1947. Around that time, he observed that there were city pioneers still living who actively worked to establish Prince George in its early years. Those in need of a place to live had used the former city hospital as a bit of a sanctuary, but they lacked the ability to sustain themselves. A.B. Moffat declared "They are killing themselves with the frying pan."[31]   He began advocating on their behalf to the Board of Trade[32], asking that a home for the aged and indigent be established. He particularly wanted that to be in a building surrounded with large grounds where they could garden. Their numbers were ten within the city with eight living in the Cariboo and another 16 scattered in the northern regions. His motion at the Board of Trade passed with a unanimous vote.[33]

GOLD PANNING FOR PRINCESS MARGARET

---

[31] This was a reference to their unchanging cuisine – frying up potatoes and eggs.

[32] A.B. Moffat was a past President of the Board of Trade, serving in 1933.

[33] "Home For Aged Supported By Board Of Trade," 6 March 1947, front page.

It was during 1955 when A.B. Moffat began to experience problems with his health. Around that time, an eye tooth became infected and the infection settled into his sinuses. That was a painful condition causing severe headaches, an inconvenient affliction which plagued him all his life. He sought treatment at the Mayo Clinic in Rochester, Minnesota.

GOLD PANNING FOR PRINCESS MARGARET

At the beginning of September, 1955 the newspaper featured a terse announcement that A.B. Moffat had been diagnosed the week before with what was termed a "minor" heart ailment. His physician advised him to take six weeks off to rest and recover.[34]

Alex Bohannan Moffat died at 72, on January 24, 1963. The three race horses he owned were passed down to Harold and to Martin Caine. After that, both men got more involved with horses, and eventually gravitated towards the standard-bred horses.

---

[34] "A.B. Moffat Confined With Heart Ailment," Prince George Citizen, 1 September 1955, front page.

Chapter III

Childhood Years
Harold Alexander Moffat (Born 24 September 1915)

Earliest Recollections

Harold attended King George V elementary school. His first teacher was Miss Milligan, a woman he remembers as being quite mean. Teachers normally got married after they came to work in Prince George, but not this one, because of her undesirable personality.

When the Moffat family moved to the Central District, there was a change of school with living in a new neighbourhood. Harold attended the two-room Central Fort George School which housed Grades 1 to 4 and 5 to 8 in each room. He began attending there at Grade 3. Desks were cast iron with wooden tops, arranged in rows. Harold remembers that the teacher's name was Miss Mowat and that it was a much happier environment for a young lad. There were about 40 boys and girls – including big boys who had come in from the country to take some courses.

Harold's Dad had a Chevrolet 490 – an open touring car – which was a bit of a novelty in a city which had few automobiles during the 1920s. As many as seventeen people at a time used to hitch rides in and on it, clinging to the hood, and standing on the running boards. Some other citizens who owned a car then were Judge Robertson, a neighbour down the street who travelled the region hearing cases at assize courts and the Styles family whose daughter, Helen, would become Harold's wife.

Drama can come into children's lives from unexpected sources. A vivid memory was the occasion when a surveyor from Fredericton, New Brunswick named Fred Burden was travelling up the Cariboo trail with legendary teamster, Al Young. They stopped at the Moffat farm, regaling everyone with a story about how the horse pulling their stage coach had lost its bridle and become more difficult to control.

Later on, the Burden family also settled in Central and had a big livery barn and a cow. Harold remembers playing baseball behind that barn. Other childhood pastimes were running hoops and rolling tires. Children often went up to a place called Deans' Heights (now called the cutbanks) and let the tires roll into the river. A favourite game was Duck on the Rock – played by choosing a large rock as the target, and then each child used his own rock in an attempt to bowl the target rock over.

Hockey was the favourite children's outdoor winter activity. As soon as the cold arrived, a field was flooded with water from the river to make an ice rink. Before the Second World War, blades and hockey boots were purchased separately. It was possible to get a new pair of work boots each fall and then have the blades attached for the winter, thus getting a dual purpose wearing from them.   Most people bought their skate blades at The Northern.

Other children's amusements included activities provided through social organizations. There was a "Good Cheer" club.[35]   Once a month, a bridge tournament was held.   Harold declared "By twelve years old, we were proficient bridge players."   Scouts was organized to meet once a week and was led by the Anglican priest, Rev. Pollinger, who later became Archbishop.   In the summers, the camp out was held at Salmon Valley.   The group was transported by freight truck.   Dick Horsefield took the troop down the Crooked River.

Harold recalls that he spent a lot of time outside the home as a youngster.   "I was six or seven years older than the rest, so it was not too long before I was more away than at home."   He remembers seeing his mother pushing a baby buggy along Nechako Drive.   His brother Keith, and two younger brothers were down on the river fishing on the rocks.   This was an era when children had a great deal of freedom and had the advantage of being able to do things independently and roam outside.

"We created all our own entertainment." Favourite areas to hike were Deans' Heights and also to a place called the Lone Tree.   They got

---

[35] The popularity of the Good Cheer Club is evidenced by its longevity. It operated through the decades, most recently headed by Bea Dezell.

there from downtown by walking across the Cameron Street bridge.

On school days, there was a one and a half hour period allotted for lunch, so children commonly came home. In that era, the main meal of the day in most families was served at noon.

People had to brave the cold to enjoy wintertime activities. The clothing of that era was not warm like that now available for children. All kids had breeches in the winter, and their mothers knit wool sweaters to go with them. Harold remembers playing hockey against a South Fort George team. By the time the game was over, he was too cold to get his skates unlaced, and ended up walking home in his skates. Stepping through snow, it wasn't too difficult, he says. In those days, Jack Duncan at Prince George Motors sharpened everybody's skates.

Central Fort George's water supply was pumped from the Nechako River and held in a water tower built to replace one that had burned. It had the word "Resurgam"[36] (Latin for 'I will rise again.') emblazoned in large letters on it. Very few homes had running water. Among the families which did were the Moffats, Robertsons, Hills, Burdens and the Central Store. They were close enough to have piped-in water from the community-owned water supply.

---

[36] "Resurgam" was the name of the first sea-going, mechanically-powered submarine. It was launched from Liverpool November 26, 1879 but sank February 25, 1880 off the coast of Wales.

Other homes had water delivered to containers stored in kitchens. In rural areas, water barrels were delivered to homes by truck in the warm weather months and by sleigh in the winter.

From the time he was six or seven years old, Harold spent his summers visiting with his Grandfather at the farm south of Quesnel. This became the regular summer routine. He went for the beginning of the haying season to help out, and stayed until it was finished. They would first put the hay down on the farm, and then do the hay on the mountains. It was stored by stacking it up in piles, carefully rounding the stacks to shed the water. Some was in the lofts in the barn, but most had to be kept outside. It was an all-summer job, accomplished with help from neighbours with two or three wagons working. His Grandfather had a large ranch of 200 to 300 acres, (and later had a smaller one of 30 to 40 acres). The experience was a defining experience for Harold because that was how he came to like horses.

Uncle Henry took over the big ranch and looked after it with his children. The family members presently in charge of the ranch are members of the fourth generation from the founder, Harry Henry Moffat.

As a young boy, Harold travelled to the farm from Prince George by river boat. There were two boats operating called the "Rounder" and the "Circle W" which gave a free ride down the river. The type of boat was similar to a twenty foot runabout with a canopy over it.

Once Harold got to make the trip down to the ranch with a famous teamster, Al Young, who ran the stage line. They drove in an old Buick. The trip was over a gravel and mud road. Hardtop didn't come until after Premier W.A.C. Bennett and Highways Minister Gaglardi paved the province. Hardtop didn't reach Ashcroft until the 1950s.

Another transportation experience was being on the BX Express. Harold knows he got to do that, but doesn't remember it well. The venerable old stern-wheeler stopped its runs up and down the river in 1921, the same year that the province experienced an economic depression.

Harold spent most summers in his younger years at his Grandfather's farm. When he was old enough to be a scout, his Dad would travel down to pick him up from the farm so he could attend scout camp at Salmon Valley.

In town, there were lots of friends. Harold recalls Bill Peters and his brother, Tom, who lived next door. Also Bud Burden, Irving Hill, the Mullet Brothers–Chuck and Edgar, Carl Wedemeyer, Gordon Hunter, George Milger, Harry and Keith Peters, Dunc Munro and a Chinese family who lived over the bridge and made a living in market garden. Their names were Li Kau and Lai Choi.

The neighbourhood boys fished and hunted together nearly every week.

May and June were lazy free days if the weather was good. The favourite pastime was to go swimming in the gravel pit. There was never any worry. The polio scare wasn't a huge concern, and only one family in South Fort George was ever affected.

Harold did spend one summer in quarantine with scarlet fever. But, he sneaked out of the house. He remembers making whistles and flutes out of willow sticks and then sitting on the river bank. The health of the community was overseen by Dr. Ewert as Health Inspector and Mrs. Bond as the school nurse.

Entertainment and information about events outside came from listening to the radio for news. The Citizen newspaper got telegrams daily. Another big event was Hockey on Saturday nights. Harold was always busy and spent time clearing Moore's Meadows and helping build the ski hills.

Boys' summers involved playing baseball and playing "flies and grounders." There was also playing marbles – "allies" – in the schoolyard and a special favourite was "duck on a rock" – involving using ball-shaped rocks to dislodge one set atop a larger stone.

In those years, children were in good shape physically, and played games according to the seasons. They built forts from snow in winter. Harold remembers a man, Bruce Douglas, who was huge in stature and had the ability to "throw a snowball like a bullet."

High School Years

There was an established tradition in the Moffat family for going away for further schooling. In 1909, Harold's father had ridden a horse to Ashcroft, and then travelled by train to Vancouver for his high school education. But, he became discouraged once he found out that it would take four years to learn French and Latin. He wanted to get telegraphy training. Harold's sister attended the Sprott Shaw business school in Vancouver.

But, secondary school education was available in Prince George by the time Harold was old enough. He attended Baron Byng High School – a four room school with about 25 to 30 in each class, covering grades 9 to 12. His most vivid memories are of the courses he loved – Geography, Literature and Maths. But, he hated French. He even recalls beating up on the French kid in the class! However, he said that "Once passing Latin and French, it gave me the feeling there wasn't anything I couldn't do!"

The reasons Harold particularly enjoyed Algebra and Geography had something to do with the influence of other people. First, the teacher. He was lucky to have a good teacher, Blair Dixon, and a friend, Howard Alexander, who changed his perspective on Math. Howard acted as a mentor and a tutor, and inspired Harold to enjoy the logic and the challenge of it.

HAROLD MOFFAT POSES IN A NEW SUIT

This was an era when people in high school had been told by their fathers that this city was the crossroads of the province. They grew up believing Prince George would eventually experience a boom and grow larger than Edmonton, Alberta. This was an idea firmly believed by parents, and Harold remembers having it instilled in him that this area would be a place of promise.

Early Work

Depression times made the economy uncertain. Harold Moffat remembers being called home to help in the store while various staff were away on holiday. Once, he was particularly pleased to be paid in merchandise. After working for two weeks he was presented with a .22 rifle.

Of his contemporaries, he remembers that other children went on to university – like Sid Perry – who became a pharmacist. Ivan Anderson became a bookkeeper at a mill. Others worked for their fathers or for the lumber camps or the railroad. Harold knew his future employment was secure in the family hardware business.

He graduated from high school in 1934. After spending eight years in elementary school and five years in high school, he was 19 when he finished school and took his up full time work at the Northern Hardware.

Chapter IV

Marriage and Family

Harold says he saw the girl he liked when she was ten. Her name then was Helen Styles, and when they grew up, he married her.

As youngsters, they knew a woman named Mrs. Williams who was like a mother to them all. They spent weekends visiting her and her two boys at West Lake. As a group they went everywhere together. Harold started going out with Helen, and he was the first of his group to get married. Dunc Munro was the last.

Today, whenever Helen meets up with some of her childhood friends, they get together and say, "Helen, we lived in the best of days." In a 1997 interview, she recalled some of those memories and the beginning years of her relationship with Harold:

> We all had Hallowe'en night – all the girls would run around the whole west end from what you would know as the Bypass up to as far as Ospika. That whole section was our playground, really. There were people by the name of Mullets that had a toffee pull. Now, Public Health wouldn't let that!! There was lovely amber toffee on these hooks – we all buttered our hands and pulled on it.

A lady called Mrs. Hurtubise lived near the corner of Fifth Avenue and Carney. She was a stout lady who must have been a confectioner in England. When we got to her house on Hallowe'en the whole table was covered with delightful sweets – stuffed dates, everything. Nobody ever took the lion's share. Our life was so free.

I met Harold at Central Fort George School. We had a lot of winter activities around the neighbourhood. At the corner of Hammond and Lyon streets, parents kept an outdoor skating rink flooded. The Moffats lived in that log house on Hammond Street, and that little hill is where we did all our sleigh riding.

Next to our school was a pink building which was the original school. The Community Association used it as a community hall. That's where the Good Cheer Club originated. They put on community dances. Harold didn't do any of those things. He didn't go dancing. He was never interested in learning how to dance. He always thought it was such a terrific waste of energy. He used to say you'd be better to hike to Hixon. I used to say, "You really should learn how to dance, it is such fun." And, he had such a good sense of rhythm. He never learned to swim. He tried, but he and his friend just never learned. We took them out to the lake eventually and really, they just went nose down. I don't know whether they didn't have any buoyancy. They weren't afraid – they were adults. I used to say, "Just put your hands out in front of you and you will float. You may go down for a minute but you'll come right back up." But, they went right down with their noses in the mud! So, we decided it wasn't any fun.[37]

MARSHALL WELLS STORE

Like most boys, Harold was more interested in baseball – but he also liked to play auction bridge. At point in their lives, as teenagers

---

[37] Interview with Helen Moffat, 23 July 1997.

in 1934, they were all just friends and had yet to
become a couple. Helen remembers the
sequence of that development with crystal
clarity:

> Harold always said he never had
> another girl. He might have gone to the
> show with his friend, Duncan's sister.
> But he always seemed to know that I
> was the person who was going to marry
> him. So, when my family left Central
> Fort George to move back downtown, I
> was 17, and I wanted to dance. I kind
> of grew away from Harold.

> We were always friends and I worked at
> Marshall Wells, and his chum Duncan
> Munro worked there. He and Harold
> were always inseparable. They used to
> fish and do all these things together.
> He would come into Marshall Wells
> when I was at the typewriter. But, I
> wanted to have a good time. I wanted to
> date. He gave me a long line and let me
> do all these things. Which I did. All
> this time he was curling and playing
> baseball and fishing and hunting.

> Harold would come down with Duncan
> and my sister and I and we played
> bridge. I just remember at one point in
> my life thinking to myself that if
> anybody had ever told me I was going to
> marry Harold I would have said, "No
> way." But, all of a sudden, he just
> seemed such an honourable person. I

remember reading that love comes up and slaps you in the face! That was certainly the reaction. I had gone out with lots of other boys and he and his pals would come by once in a while and we'd go to the show or something.

STYLES FAMILY HOME IN ONTARIO

Eventually I started to date him quite seriously. We were engaged New Year's of 1938 and we had planned to be married the next spring, but there was a terrible flu epidemic that winter. All my family got sick. I was still living at home but working. I had a younger sister and brother – my Mom had twins – after the youngest of us four was ten. So, I remember being home looking after all these people and eventually I got the flu and I got a really, really bad ear infection and ended up with a mastoid infection. In those days, that meant going to Vancouver because there were no qualified specialists – just GPs – and I had surgery. I left in February and didn't get home until the end of May. I agreed it wasn't a wise thing to do to get married when my health was not really fully recovered. So we waited another year.[38]

Popular Couple Married Here
Helen Styles Becomes Bride Of Harold Moffat At Quiet Ceremony

Two of Prince George's most popular young people were united in marriage Wednesday afternoon, March 8, when Helen Maurine Styles, second daughter of Mr. and Mrs. E.W. Styles of this city, became the bride of Harold Alexander Moffat, eldest son of Mr. and Mrs. A.B. Moffat, also of this city. Rev. G.B. Punter of Vanderhoof performed the ceremony. The wedding was solemnized quietly at the home of the bride's parents, and was witnessed only by relatives and intimate friends of the young couple. The bride, who entered to the strains of the Wedding March played by Mrs. R. Yardley, was attractively gowned in navy crepe with hat to match, and wore a corsage of roses and lilies-of-the-valley. Miss Mary Snell, her only attendant, chose rust

---

[38] Ibid.

crepe with hat to match.   Mr. Duncan Munroe supported the groom.

Following the ceremony an informal reception was held when the young couple received the congratulations of their friends, standing beneath the wedding arch of evergreen interlaced with spring flowers.

Later they left by car on a brief honeymoon, and on their return will take up residence in this city.

Prior to the wedding, numerous showers were held in compliment to the bride-elect.[39]

Harold was 24 years old when he married. By then, he worked in the store full time for $83.00 a month. He was able to afford his first house as the result of a legacy from his grandfather, who put $100 into a savings bond when Harold was born in 1915. By 1939, it had grown to be worth $500 to $600. Harold used $300 of that to buy the first house, and furnished it with the balance.

Their first home was on Calgary Street, which has since been renamed Alward. It didn't have a house number because the city was small enough that people knew where everyone lived. Typical of many houses then, it had been moved to that site and was a comfortable little home with a kitchen and living room and dining room

---

[39] The Prince George Citizen, Thursday, 9 March 1939, p. 8.

and two bedrooms, but no bathroom. An extension off the kitchen later was renovated to install a shower and a toilet but not a bathtub. At first, the house had no hot water, just cold water taps. Harold accomplished those alterations himself.

The house had a trap door in the kitchen ceiling with a rope on it. It was right over top of the wood and coal kitchen stove. During winter, the trap door had to be kept opened to let the heat up to keep the pipes that went across to the shower and the toilet from freezing. Insulation wasn't enough to keep the cold out so over the winter months frost covered the door hinges. There were no storm doors. The kitchen door opened to the outside.

A wood heater kept the living room warm. Both the heater and kitchen stove had to be kept going all night to maintain some warmth. We had to keep them going all night. The work involved in staying warm seemed endless.

We often used to wonder why winter seemed so long! We now recognize we were exhausted! We didn't get our rest. You had to sit up. This great long stove pipe was in the wall – it would heat to red hot, so you couldn't go to bed in case the place would catch fire. But, you had to open the dampers. We never got our rest. We finally got an automatic oil heater. We thought we'd died and gone to heaven. To set that thing at night and get up in the morning and the house was as warm as when you went to bed. That was wonderful. We were in that house for ten years from 1939 to 1949.[40]

Canada joined in the Second World War in September 1939. That meant shortages and rationing of food like sugar, meat, and butter. Just two weeks before their March 8th wedding, Harold had sustained a serious injury – dislocating his shoulder when he slammed into the boards playing hockey. That caused significant pain and compromised the range of motion in his arm for years afterwards. Unable to enlist, Harold became actively involved with the Home Guard during the war which helped enforce blackouts and reduce the potential for being targetted by enemy bombers. The Home Guard toured around at night checking for chinks of light. Windows of houses had rolls of tarpaper fastened inside on casters making it easy to pull them down and seal the shade tightly at the bottom.

Thousands of American troops came through Prince George in 1942 when the Alaska Highway was built. The American government built the highway on Canadian soil as a strategic military supply line to Alaska. The project involved 11,000 troops and 16,000 civilians over an eight month period from March to October. There were more soldiers than citizens living in Prince George for much of that time.

---

[40] Interview with Helen Moffat, 23 July 1997.

Harold met a lot of the Canadian servicemen as they came through town There were young boys from the Oxford rifles, many from Ontario towns like Oxford, Windsor, and Ingersoll. The Moffat home became something of a home-away-from-home for many of them. That living room was a welcome respite from the hot tents and mosquitoes in the army camp.

Soldiers would hike down to the Moffat house and express appreciation for being able to sit on a chesterfield and for countless meals. They ate Helen's coconut cream pies and played cribbage, sometimes staying there until 3:00 in the morning.   Entertainment came from conversation and singing around the family's player piano. That was the same instrument Helen's father-in-law, A.B. Moffat, bought her. He got it from Mrs. Watson, who brought it with her to Prince George on the steamboats. They had the rolls for all the old songs.

The piano helped that first married home seem a lively place. For a while, a nursing sister came and stayed with the family. She had trained with Helen's sister at the Royal Columbian Hospital and Helen invited her to stay. Harold claims that she spoiled his son in the years she lived there. Harold and Helen had two children, a son (Edward Alexander) and a daughter (Marilyn Patricia) while living in their first house.

The Moffats moved to their next and permanent home at 2340 Laurier Crescent in February 1950. That house was built, financed with a 20-year mortgage which was paid off in 1970 at $72.00 per month. Daughter Valerie Jean was born in 1951. Those were busy years, happily remembered:

> I always knew I wanted to have one more child. I got involved in PTA and the Eastern Star, which is associated with the Masonic Fraternity. I always knew that I would like to take office, and I did have a lot of offices, and then they got to the stage where they wanted me to go through the chairs. But, I kind of hedged and said I didn't really want to, but they insisted that I go. What I wanted to say was I didn't want to do it because I wanted to have another baby. But I didn't want to make that public announcement before I was even pregnant. So, I took it, but right after that, I set out to have Valerie. It took me twelve years to have three children. There are four years between Ted and Marilyn and then there's eight years between Marilyn and Valerie. So it was like raising two families because a lot of the mores changed by the time Valerie was a teenager. When she was eight, Marilyn was 16. By the time Valerie was ten, Marilyn had gone nursing. So, she was raised like an only child. Not only that, the whole era changed.

I remember when Ted graduated, there were 70 children in the class. When Valerie graduated, there were 700. When Ted and Marilyn graduated, I knew all the children and their parents. And I knew what kind of home they had. When Valerie graduated, I didn't know any of the 700 – and didn't have a "handle" on the kind of people she was keeping company with. I had to police much more diligently, without being ruthless. It was a different experience.

I wanted to call her Valerie Jean because I liked the sound of it, and I have a very dear friend, Jean, whom Harold and I met in the early years of our marriage. We met Jean and Bill Fleming. Bill was at that time working for CNR, Jean was pregnant and we had our first babies together. Both of our boys played ball on the same team. We used to go down to where the Northern Hardware warehouse now is. That's where they played ball. There were no bleachers, no seats, no concession stand. We went with a blanket and a packet of sandwiches and a jug of juice. Subsequently, after we each had two children (a boy and a girl each), I was one of the lucky ones because I had Harold's store truck to sit in. One day, I saw this red-headed girl was sitting on a log, and she was so obviously pregnant, and sitting out in the hot sun. I asked "Would you like to come and sit with me in the truck?" "Would I ever," she said. So, we became friends and she invited us back to their apartment. They lived, to start with, in the apartments up over the store that Mr. Moffat had originally. And we became friends. That was another nice thing about our early years of marriage was that we had lots of good friends. My neighbours helped me raise my children and I guess I helped my neighbours raise their children.[41]

There are dramatic stories in all families about the challenges of raising children. Helen had one that was miraculous for the fact that it didn't have a tragic ending:

I remember when Ted was in junior high, about 12 years old. He went on a hike with a teacher, Mr. Beauselais who took them across on the riverbanks that are now beyond Fort George Park. They were running along the top of the bank. When Ted went to do it, I guess he was in the rear, and the bank gave way and he plummeted down onto this sand bank. Probably, he really stunned himself. The tragedy was that the teacher didn't notice he was missing. A few minutes later, he said, "Look, there's Ted Moffat walking along the railway tracks." But, he was going the

---

[41] Ibid.

wrong way, he was walking in the direction out of town. Poor Mr. Beausolais nearly had a heart attack!

They jumped over and ran down the bank. They were lucky enough to find Ted's glasses sticking out of the sand. It was a real miracle when I think about it in retrospect, that he didn't break his neck. We were going that night to a graduation, and Harold was going to be the speaker. He was rushing around getting bathed and shaved and dressed and Ted came home. He came in the door and said, "Momma, I fell down in the mud." I said, "Oh, Ted, did you hurt yourself?" "Not really," came the answer. I told him not to worry about his clothes – just to take them off and leave them by the door. I looked at him and he appeared fine.

The next morning, Mr. Beausolais appeared at my door wanting to know how Ted was. I said, "He's okay, was there any reason?" He said, "Oh, Mrs. Moffat, he had the worst fall. He tumbled several feet down off this cliff. I should have come last night." I told him Harold had to speak at the graduation so we had to go out. Well, I sent Ted to school. If there was anything wrong, I didn't think you could walk around with a broken neck. The doctor said, yes, it was possible, and

Ted should be checked out. He did and said everything seemed to be okay.

Later, we discovered that farther down, below where they'd taken the x-ray, there was a damaged area quite close to the spine. It surfaced when Ted got into Senior High. He was going to school and working at the store and doing a lot of lifting. We finally had it checked out and I'm sure it was a part of that. Anyway, the story had a happy ending.

While Marilyn was in Brownies, all the activities she attended meant getting there on foot. Helen didn't drive, and she didn't have a car available to her during the day even if she could. In order to earn the merit badge called "The Golden Hand," Marilyn had to cook carrots and make a blancmange. Once she had the dishes ready, they had to be taken to the Brown Owl's home in the Millar Addition. Mother and daughter came up with an inspired way to transport the food. They borrowed a baby buggy and walked it over to have her effort examined. Streets weren't paved so it was a gruelling trip pushing along through gravel, dust dirt in the heat of the day. Helen remembered thinking, "Oh my, it's quite a thing to be a mother." She admits to the thought that it isn't the Brownies who should get the Golden Hand, it's the mothers!

The Moffat family had a place at Six Mile Lake. They would go there every summer, and it was like a pioneer existence – no running water and harder work. Harold's father drove back and forth to the store. A.B. Moffat liked to take Ted in to the store with him on Sundays, while working on the deposits.

Ted got a taste of earning his own money by getting a newspaper route delivering the Prince George Citizen. He had to buy the papers in advance and then collect from customers at the end of the month. Ted also was a Boy Scout and a member of the first Ranger group. He and his friends organized the Rangers. Marilyn was a Girl Guide, but Valerie didn't get into that.

Marilyn attended Prince George High School. She had the fun of being elected Homecoming Queen on Friday, November 4th, 1960.[42] The other girls in the running for the title were Pat Torgerson, Adina Thony and Terry Takeda. It was a short rule, and meant presiding over the homecoming celebrations that Friday evening held in the High School fieldhouse.

While her children were young, Helen taught piano lessons—popular music—in their home to students after school.

Harold made sure that his children spent their summer holidays at the store. They learned to do everything that was required in that enterprise, as part of the "regular Moffat upbringing." Eventually, their career paths took shape with Ted moving into a lifelong career with

---

[42] "Marilyn Moffat Elected Homecoming Queen Here," Prince George Citizen, 7 November 1960, front page.

the store, Marilyn becoming a nurse, and Valerie a teacher.

Both girls lived at home until they were married. Marilyn worked in Hawaii as a nurse for a year, and then came home to work at Prince George Regional Hospital. She has now retired from her work as a recovery room nurse. Valerie taught at Mackenzie and eventually made her home in Prince George while teaching at Blackburn. She now works as a teacher/librarian for Prince George Secondary School.

It is always interesting to hear what a wife has to say about her husband. When asked what Harold considers most important in life, Helen confidently responded: "His wife and family, and the store, and then the horses."

Asked to look back over their long, happy years together she speaks of her husband affectionately and with unswerving loyalty:

> Harold was always community-minded. He was for years on the school board and he did that without pay. He considers it a mistake that they ever started to pay them. He thinks it should be something people want to do because they're interested in children and their education.

> Anything else he did, like work on the Industrial Development Commission when he was interested in the pulp mills, he did out of interest. At the time

business was solely dependent on logging and when the big strike came on, the town nearly folded up because there was nothing to sustain it. We needed other industry and Harold was very much aware of that.

That was a terrible, awful scourge of a vendetta that BCTV did.[43] It was a terrible thing, really. I can remember Harold and I sitting on the chesterfield watching those programs and feeling totally defenceless against something like that. The reporter viciously said "Harold Moffat wouldn't talk to us." I used to say I would like to meet the person who would be brave enough to approach Harold to do something that would be anything but truthful. I can't imagine anybody ever being brave enough! It was unfortunate that nobody ever took the trouble to find out whether it was a true story or an untrue story before going on air. It was a terrible experience and I always admired Harold so immensely because he didn't become vindictive.

Although Harold sued he said "I don't want any money. I don't want anything.

---

[43] Refers to a series of reports broadcast on BCTV's The News Hour in March 1977 which precipitated a law suit and an on-air apology to Harold Moffat. Details provided at the end of Chapter VII – In the Mayor's Chair.

I want a public apology. I want my integrity restored. That's all I ask."

The case was finally going to court in 1979. That summer, Harold had an accident at the barn. He had this old truck. They were over at the coffee shop. Harold was sitting on the back of the truck. The fellow who was driving the truck had kicked the mat out of the way and hit the gas pedal, and the truck took off at the top of the Esso station. Harold fell off and hit his head on the pavement and fractured his skull and ended up in the hospital. This case was to come up in October. I was just sick because I worried if his memory would be sharp enough. Almost the night before it was supposed to go to trial, Mr. Parrett phoned and said, "BCTV want to settle out of court and I have demanded this public apology. It had to be printed in a number of papers and read on BCTV during the 6:00 news."

Now, it's an apology but it's a poor one. That was a moment when I thought Harold really showed his true grit. He could have become bitter and antisocial because it destroyed his integrity and all that he worked for, the free will out of the kindness of his heart and all the things that he did.[44]

---

[44] Ibid.

Chapter V

School Board Service

Harold Moffat served 23 years as a School Trustee for School District No. 57 from 1943 to 1966; and for three of those years as Chairman

British Columbia's modern school districts were created as a result of recommendations of the Cameron Report of 1945 which reorganized the province's 650 school districts into 74. It was the single most dramatic organizational change which occurred in the Department of Education in a quarter century. Maxwell Cameron had been appointed by the provincial government to conduct a one-man inquiry into the issues surrounding educational organization and finance.

The report's recommendations allowed:

1. That the administration of education through local school boards be retained;
2. That a Provincial programme of education, defined in financial terms, be made available throughout British Columbia by means of a grant system requiring equal tax rates on all property;

3. That adequate local units or school districts be created wherever in the Province they do not already exist.[45]

Each of the new school districts was to include a major population centre which would then be designated as the site of the secondary school for that district. In School District No. 57 – that was Prince George.

From the early years, Mayor Patterson[46] ran the School Board. There are no records extant of those early years, although some recall that minutes were taken by Harry Greensell until Irving Moss became the Board's secretary.

Mayor Patterson is remembered by Harold as a very prudent School District manager. Within their social group an opinion was formed that there should be a change at city hall. They decided to get some younger people to run.

Dr. H.J. Hocking had been a member of the School Board since 1936. He approached Harold in 1942 and said, "Moffat, if you go for school trustee, I'll go for alderman."[47] They did that, and the election results put Harold Moffat in as a trustee beginning in January 1943.[48] Dr. Hocking was not elected alderman.

---

[45] Maxwell A. Cameron, Report of the Commission of Inquiry into Educational Finance, 1945, p. 39.

[46] A.M. Patterson was Prince George's longest-serving mayor. He was elected first in 1927 and served continuously until the end of 1944.

[47] Remark recalled in a conversation with Harold Moffat, 1 February 1996.

[48] Harold Moffat was elected Chairman of the School Trustees for 1945; and again in 1951, and in 1956.

That was an exciting time to be involved in education. There was a strong sense of importance attached to planning for the future. Prince George was going to get a new school, Prince George Senior Secondary School, to replace Baron Byng, the old high school which had been built just below King George V Elementary School.

Contemplating the new building opened up the chance to get something for the community – a badly needed meeting hall and performance venue. The only buildings that existed in the mid-Forties of any size were the old Army huts. School Inspector Harold Stafford wanted a community centre for plays – and a place for students to play basketball.

Harold, from his position on school board, set out to make sure that PGSSS would be a community-oriented school. It was one of the first schools built after the war. It cost $186,000. The local School Board successfully presented the case to the provincial government and the school was expanded from the original plan of six classrooms to eight.

Some important political lobbying began on behalf of the Prince George School District. First, Inspector Stafford invited the BC School Trustees' Association to hold a convention in Prince George.[49] At the time the invitation was extended, about 75 to 80 delegates were

---

[49] The 1951 Prince George convention was the first time the BCSTA held a convention outside the Lower Mainland.

expected. The convention attracted more than 400 – overwhelming the available hotel space and causing a scramble to billet the visitors.

H.B. King was the Chief Inspector of Schools for British Columbia and his son, Hub King, practised law in Prince George. The son helped encourage his father to visit, which he did. More influence came from Harry Perry, a former Prince George Mayor, who served then as Education Minister.[50]

Those officials pooled their influence and with a great deal of local support from the Jaycees, helped put the vote through for the new school. Construction began and was nearing completion in 1944. The official opening occurred the first week in January 1945.

With the school nearing completion, it needed to be furnished. That task fell to the three Harolds: Harold Stafford and Harold Pennington (serving then as the high school principal) went with School Board Chairman Harold Moffat to Vancouver to look at modern furnishings for high schools. (Stafford was principal at Kitsilano High School in Vancouver.) Harold Moffat recalled that it was the first time he had ever seen students moving about between classes instead of staying in the same room all day with various subject teachers coming to the room.

---

[50] Harry Perry was Mayor of Prince George for 1917, 1918 and again in 1920. He was elected MLA for the riding of Fort George serving from 1920 to 1928 and from 1933 to 1946. He was Minister of Education from 1941 to 1945.

It was at this time that attention got paid to recruiting a principal for the new school. School Inspector Harold Stafford offered to interview prospective principals in Vancouver on behalf of the Prince George School District. The local school board received a telegram outlining attributes of the various candidates.

This was the beginning of the Industrial Arts era, and the person suggested as most suitable was Ray Williston, who was then studying in Ontario. He was hired as the one with best knowledge of the new Industrial Arts field and also because he would be qualified to serve as supervising principal of the new large area.

Ray Williston arrived here by train in 1946. Harold Moffat picked him up at the station. He couldn't have known it then, but the person he went to meet that day would become a life-long family friend.

Harold drove Ray Williston to the Prince George Hotel and tried to get him a room but the place was full. That's how the new principal ended up sleeping on a cot in the hallway.

The recommendations of the Cameron Report, released in 1945, were beginning to be put in place by 1946. Williston became Supervising Principal of all the schools in the District. When the modern School Board was formed in 1946, it was re-named School District No. 57, and the existing school assets became property of the new district.

For years, Prince George's progress in education was held back because of the inability to offer things that were available in other parts of the province, like dormitories. The situation for students who lived outside town was less than ideal. Arrangements were made for them to billet with families living near the schools, but most were expected to work for their keep. A survey was taken and the results indicated high interest in moving into a dormitory situation once that became available.

Harold decided to act. He knew that there were old Army barracks available, complete with kitchens. He had some moved to a block of land on Alward Street and they were operating within a few months. Since acquiring the buildings was being done without official government approval, the School District had no authority to spend any money. Harold and fellow School Trustee John Nilson had to approach the bank to secure initial operating money. The bank manager listened to Harold's pitch and said "If you don't get approval, you and Nilson will be operating a boarding house up there." All went smoothly.

The District's first school dormitories were two 90-foot long buildings with a centre connecting piece forming an "H" shape which was the dining hall. The beds came with it – former army cots. When it came time to move in, Harold Moffat, Ray Williston and Jack Beech packed in all the furniture and stoves.

ELIZABETH YOST

Suites were created in each dormitory as teacherages. That way, dormitory supervisor and matron, Mrs. Elizabeth Yost, had some help maintaining discipline. Other teachers lived in the former army hospital, located off Alward near the site of Prince George Regional Hospital's employee parking lot. That two-story building housed three teachers and their families downstairs and six single teachers upstairs.

Eventually, the government put up half the funding needed for the dormitory. It was the first operated by a public school board in B.C.

The next shortage which had to be addressed was a bit trickier to solve – the lack of enough teachers. Harold went to talk to the Alberta trustees at a meeting in Red Deer about their recruiting methods and discovered that they were into overseas recruitment.

After that, Harold made a presentation to the B.C. teachers. He sent a letter to the Agent-General for British Columbia in London to get an ad placed for overseas teachers. Requests came by cable for application forms. Forms were sent by cable, and printed in London for distribution there.

Applications started coming in. So many arrived that a system had to be set up to vet the applications. The roster of applicants was provided to outlying areas around the north with the intent to let them have first choice of the applicants. Many did come from England to teach here, though some preferred to be in the Lower Mainland and moved there eventually.

Harold claims that the Prince George school district "invented" the portable school. An example was the need for a school building and teacherage at Telachek. The provincial government allowed that a school could be created whenever there were twelve children of school age within a three-mile radius.

Portable buildings got constructed inexpensively. They were put on skids and taken to the land that someone had offered for a school. There, the portables would be rested on a log foundation. The school and teacherage could be moved to the next location as needed. During the 1950s, sawmills were being started in lots of remote places around Prince George. That drove the decision of where the next school would be needed.

The Assistant Superintendent of Schools came up here and discovered the "discrepancies" that had gone on. George Milburn was then government agent in Prince George. Spike Enemark had the contract to move the old army buildings which were beginning to find new life as school houses starting in 1949. Harold asserts "They were a Godsend for kids out in the country."[51]

The grant for schools was based on an asset value. In Prince George, the School District managed to build a school and teacherage for less than any place anywhere else was able to build even the school.

A special meeting was called for June 17, 1949 to deal with Ray Williston's resignation as Senior Principal due to his appointment as Inspector of Schools. The position was offered to Jack Beech, who had been groomed by Williston to take his place. Beech accepted.

---

[51] Interview with Harold Moffat, 7 November 1995.

HAROLD MOFFAT OVERSEES SCHOOL INSPECTORS BEDDING DOWN

During a November 1949 meeting, Trustee Moffat reported on the growth of the District since its formation in 1946, outlining plans for the building program. Within three months, he was elected Chairman of the School Board's building committee. At the June 14, 1951 meeting, the trustees elected Harold Moffat again as School Board Chairman.

At the first meeting in October 1951, the trustees started with an afternoon tour of the major school properties. Those were: the high school, King George V, the high school annex, Fort George Central, Fort George South, Connaught, the dormitory and the dormitory annex buildings.

British Columbia School Trustees' Association

This

Life Membership Certificate

is presented to

Harold A. Moffat

In grateful appreciation of faithful service to the cause of Education in the Province of British Columbia during many years.

President of the British Columbia School Trustees' Association

for the year *1952*

_____
Secretary

_____
President

Dated *October 1st 1954*

BCSTA LIFE MEMBER 1952

After operating on an informal and *ad hoc* basis for a long time, it was realized that there was need to fall in line with Victoria's bureaucracy. Department officials had the power to hold back funding, and it began to be more practical to follow a building program and comply with by-laws. At a December 1953 meeting, Trustee Moffat announced that he had an appointment in Victoria the following week to have those committee details finalized.

The school board voted, effective February 1st, 1954 that henceforth, all rural and full-time janitors would thereafter be given the title "custodian" instead.

It became apparent by the next month that there had to be a better effort made to attract people into teacher training. To press the issue, Trustee Moffat and Principal Beech travelled to Victoria on behalf of the Board. At the same meeting, Inspector Williston informed the board that several definite appointments were being made of teachers from the United Kingdom. This result was from the ads Harold had placed in British publications.

An assessment was made about the operation of the dormitory during the spring of 1954. It was reported to be operating satisfactorily. An incident involving some unruly boys meant that repairs were needed to the furnace room wall and also for wall damage in the individual sleeping rooms. Those boys responsible had been assessed fines of $3.00 each.[52]

---

[52] Minutes of the School Board Special Meeting, 15 June 1954.

Asked to reflect on the usefulness of the dormitories here, Harold rates that experiment as a success overall. "Fine kids came out of the dormitory. They had a sense of family there."[53]

By the fall of 1954, school enrolment increased to the point that at King George V school, classes began operating in shifts with one group of students attending morning sessions and another in the afternoon. The dormitory space configurations changed so that three students were housed in each room with plans to revert to the standard arrangement of two students to a room as soon as more space could be provided.

At the time, the Department of Education would not authorize any building program until voters had a chance to pass a referendum. At the School District's Annual Representatives Meeting in December, Trustee Moffat spoke on behalf of the Building Committee about the space problems created by increasing student numbers in almost every school in the District. He announced that plans were being formulated to present another building program to the electors at the earliest date possible.[54] At that same meeting, a question was put forward about school closures, particularly respecting extremely cold weather. The answer given was: "The school is always open; it does not close for

---

[53] Interview with Harold Moffat, 8 February 1996.
[54] School District No. 57, Minutes of the Annual Representatives Meeting, 15 December 1954.

weather. The teacher is supposed to be on duty for one pupil."[55]

The triumphant news from the School District came at the last meeting of 1954. That was the announcement that sixteen teachers from the United Kingdom would be coming to teach in Prince George during the 1955-1956 school year.[56]

Progress on creating more classroom space was reported by Trustee Moffat in March. He announced that plans had been received from the architect for the elementary school and plans for the high school would be ready within ten days. Until construction was completed, portable classrooms would be set up on the main school site. The board chose the name for the new elementary school as "South Central Elementary School" and voted that the new senior school would be named "Prince George Senior High School."[57] By June, construction was well under way on both new schools.

An interesting aspect of school naming was under discussion that fall. The minutes reflected a shift in what had been a longstanding tradition:

> Trustee Moffat brought to the attention of the Board it was previously considered advisable to name the schools north of Summit Lake by

---

[55] Ibid.
[56] Minutes of the School Board Regular Meeting, 28 December 1954.
[57] Minutes of the School Board Regular Meeting, 8 March 1955.

number in relation to their respective mileage. The mileage is now taken from Prince George and such a method may cause confusion. The Board agreed whenever possible all new schools should be named after some significant lake or community. The building now under construction is to be officially called "Hart Lake School."[58]

In November, the School Board voted to set policy on when school buses would cease running over the winter months. The vote carried:

That it be policy to discontinue operating the school buses after 25 degrees below zero by official reading at the airport, the Secretary to arrange for regular school bus broadcast at approximately 7:15 a.m. each school day.

The temperature chosen would have been set in degrees Fahrenheit, equivalent to minus 17 degrees on the Celsius scale.[59] CKPG began broadcasting the school bus information at a cost of $20.00 per month. By mid-December, Trustee Moffat proposed that a definite time be set for that broadcast and also that an

---

[58] Minutes of the School Board Regular Meeting, 8 November 1955.
[59] By the late 1990s, School District No. 57's cold temperature policy was set at minus 35 degrees Celsius.

advertisement be inserted in The Prince George Citizen.[60]

Once again, Harold Moffat was elected School Board Chairman at the first meeting in January 1956. It was a year when the trustees' focus was on building schools. Renovations were approved in February for the King George V school and the Board hired an architect to draw up the plans.

Trustee Moffat was not present for the two April meetings (10th and 24th) – representing an unusual absence. They are among the few School Board meetings he ever missed. He had devoted the evenings of the second and fourth Tuesdays of each month for so long, it had become a habit.

He returned to resume the chair at the May 8th meeting at which reports were given about construction of the North Nechako School and discussions started about locating a suitable site in the Peden Hill area for construction of a two-room school. By mid-June of 1956, altogether there were eight schools for which tenders had been called before proceeding with construction.

During the spring of 1957, the Board was asked to consider a request from the Seventh Day Adventist church about using the Connaught School auditorium for a youth rally. The minutes record:

---

[60] Minutes of the School Board Regular Meeting, 13 December 1955.

The Board expressed the general opinion any activity to assist religious instruction of the youth outside the schools should be encouraged if possible because such activities are of a general benefit to the community. The CEO was authorized to grant permission at his discretion for the use of school facilities for youth religious activities.[61]

Renovations to the King George V school continued through August. Trustee Moffat reported on the progress and commented that although the quarry tile floor had been omitted, otherwise the specifications set out by Architect Briggs were being followed. Stucco work was proceeding on the outside and Trustee Moffat offered his opinion that the improvements and renovations, other than the floors, would render the building in better condition in 1957 than when it was first constructed.[62]

---

[61] Minutes of the School Board Regular Meeting, 30 April 1957. This position was later reversed at the January 14, 1958 School Board Regular Meeting. It was decided to inform all religious sects currently using school facilities that they would no longer be available for religious activities. The stated reason was "Established Board policy was reiterated to the effect the Board does not intend to compete with private facilities nor with the civic Center in the matter of rentals, but to assist in the promotion of cultural type local entertainment."

[62] Minutes of the School Board Regular Meeting, 26 August 1957. Construction began on the eight-room school at the corner of Edmonton Street and Seventh Avenue in 1918 and was completed in 1921. When it opened, it was named King George V school for the reigning English monarch.

During the fall meetings, the School Board wrestled with ways to deal with large numbers of students. There was special concern to eliminate double shifting at the South Central School. The records lay out the magnitude of the problem in these numbers:

1957 School Enrolments[63]

School	Enrolment	Teachers	Ratio
Connaught	641	17	37.7
Central Fort George	238	7	34.0
South Central	377	10	37.7
King George V	271	8	33.7
Millar Addition	68	2	34.0
South Fort George	157	5	31.7
Junior High School	760	33	23.0
Senior High School	395	23	17.1

By the end of November, Trustee Moffat reported communication had been received from the teachers respecting a salary agreement. He relayed the message that

> The teachers' committee has informed the Board representatives the BCTF will be circularizing all teachers recommending that they do not accept positions offering salaries below the BCTF minimum recommended salary and that this will concern some categories on the new scale.[64]

---

[63] Report submitted to School Board Regular Meeting, 10 September 1957.

[64] Minutes of the School Board Regular Meeting, 28 November 1957.

Trustee Moffat moved the resolution "That the salary committee be empowered to sign the teachers' salary schedule negotiated by the committee," which was carried.[65]

As the 1950s decade came to an end, some forward-looking decisions were championed with the School Board by Trustee Moffat. It was he who recommended that the Board support efforts to bring university extension courses to Prince George. Those courses were geared for the professional development interests of teachers wishing to improve their qualifications for holding higher teaching certificates.[66]

The province had recently appointed a Royal Commission on Education (later known as the Chant Commission) and it was decided that School District No. 57 should submit a brief. Trustee Moffat was asked to chair the committee which would prepare that document.[67] He presented it to the Commission members when it travelled to Prince George on September 14.

Over the spring and summer of 1957, the School Board considered re-naming some schools. Principal Sutherland had made a special request that South Central School be re-named[68] because that caused confusion with other similar school names (South Central,

---

[65] Ibid.

[66] Minutes of the School Board Regular Meeting, 25 March 1958.

[67] Ibid.

[68] The name "Harwin Elementary School" was selected during the April 28, 1959 School Board meeting from a list of 26 suggestions submitted by Principal Sutherland.

Central Fort and South Fort). The go-ahead was given to build Peden Hill Elementary on land owned by the city along Westwood Drive. At that point the spelling was changed from "Peedon" to reflect the accurate spelling of that pioneer family name.

The summer doldrums must have settled over the School Board because the trustees were not able to come up with alternative names and had to seek guidance from the Town Planning Board to get some suggestions. The one exception was Trustee Moffat, who moved "That the Prince George Jr. High School be renamed Duchess Park Junior High School" subject to Department approval. The motion carried.[69]

The first meeting of 1959 saw Trustee Moffat (supported by A.W. Wilson) get behind the establishment of a college. The board voted it into official policy with the wording:

> That the Board go on record regarding the need for a Junior College in this area due to the geographical situation and the number of pupils available for such a college.[70]

Six months later, he got to reinforce this by moving:

> That this Board apply to the Council of Public Instruction for the establishment of a school district college commencing

---

[69] Minutes of School Board Regular Meeting, 22 July 1958.
[70] Minutes of School Board Regular Meeting, 6 January 1959.

with the school year 1960-61 in accordance with Section 163 (1) of the Public Schools Act.[71]

A concerted effort was expended on finding teachers for this region. Trustee Moffat was appointed to a special Teacher Recruitment Committee which organized the campaign to get teachers to come to British Columbia. The committee did its work all on paper – advertising, vetting the applications and appraising their qualifications. As they arrived, they were royally welcomed and made to feel at home by Bob Gracey, who headed the welcoming committee. All around, it appeared to be a successful campaign. Harold admits "All were excellent teachers. But, they headed to Vancouver for the next year."[72]

With a view to attracting more high school students – and thus to demonstrate growing need for a community college – the School Board announced a big financial break for students. The idea was suggested and moved by Trustee Moffat:

> That commencing from September 1959 all full Senior Matriculation students be granted free tuition fees to Christmas, and thereafter based upon the Christmas examinations. Those students passing all subjects be granted free tuition for the school year; students

---

[71] Minutes of School Board Regular Meeting, 25 June 1959.
[72] Interview with Harold Moffat, 8 February 1996.

passing all but one subject be charged 50% of the full year's fees; students passing all but two subjects will be charged the full year's fees; and students failing three or more subjects be released from class." CARRIED[73]

One of the last decisions taken before 1959 closed was a vote taken "that the soft drink dispenser be removed forthwith from the Duchess Park School."[74] The School Board members' concern for nutrition clearly was very much ahead of its time.

An important administrative re-organization was effected at Trustee Moffat's suggestion during the Board's first meeting in 1960. The change he promoted, and the Board adopted, was to create an Operation Council. That body was comprised of the District Superintendent, the Secretary-Treasurer in charge of financial matters, and one other official whose responsibility was overseeing all the physical properties within the District.

During the month of February, a spate of policies concerning students and teachers got passed. Extracts from those minutes reveal the range:

"That no school in this district shall be closed because of inclement weather provided the interior of the building is warm and dry."

---

[73] Minutes of School Board Regular Meeting, 27 October 1959.
[74] Minutes of School Board Regular Meeting, 15 December 1959.

"That the Board does not approve snake parades by pupils."[75]

"That Junior High or Elementary pupils are not permitted to travel outside the district for extra curricular activities."

"That the Board will co-operate and assist in the operation of the School for Retarded Children."

"That all teachers may be required to have an annual chest X-ray."

"That maternity leaves of teachers must be at least two months—one month before the birth and one afterwards."[76]

At the next meeting the issue of purchasing a television set for the dormitory was discussed. The board concluded that this was not desirable, and therefore no policy was required.

Trustee Moffat came closer to realizing his ambition of getting UBC Extension courses offered in Prince George. Representatives from UBC, Dean Geoff Andrew and Professor Ron Baker visited in May 1960 and provided advice about mounting the program here, along with a cost estimate of about $9,000.00. It was fortunate to have an ally in Dean Andrew because he had been a champion for and staunch defender of greater accessibility to

---

[75] This was a form of amusement whereby groups of students would form a long line and "snake" through stores, generally causing a disruption. It was regarded as an annoying prank and drew stares of disapproval, especially from merchants and store clerks.

[76] Minutes of School Board Regular Meeting, 9 February 1960.

higher education. He strongly supported UBC's expansion of course offerings throughout the province.

The next month, District Superintendent Alexander read a letter to the School Board from UBC outlining that university's requirements to proceed with the plan of having one of their professors resident in Prince George. It was Trustee Moffat who proposed the motion: "That the Chairman of the Board be empowered to sign the memorandum of agreement with the university."[77] That was the beginning of university courses being offered locally.

In recognition of his prior involvement and interest in keeping the schools staffed with appropriately trained personnel, Trustee Moffat was appointed at the beginning of January 1962 to head up a special School Board committee responsible for teacher recruitment.[78] Related to that was the need to provide opportunities for teachers to upgrade their qualifications and become eligible to move through the salary ranks.

Triumph came in the area of overseas teacher recruitment by the fall of 1965. The Department of Education issued a report indicating that 95 teachers acquired positions in British Columbia as a result of overseas

---

[77] Minutes of School Board Regular Meeting, 18 June 1960.
[78] Minutes of School Board Regular Meeting, 9 January 1962.

recruitment. Of those, twenty were on staff in School District No. 57.[79]

In September, UBC President Dr. John MacDonald visited Prince George in the first year of his presidency to investigate the potential for establishing a junior college here. He met with a School Board committee comprised of trustees Moffat, Atkinson, Elliott and Rhodes who had provided him with statistics and reports concerning the District.[80]

Continuing with his dedication to recruiting teachers, Trustee Moffat attended teachers' conventions, put up booths and handed out brochures about the experience of teaching and living in Prince George. For one display, he even included a power chain saw to represent that "slice of life" that was so strongly associated with the regional economy.

Concentrating on recruiting teachers from other parts of British Columbia, Trustee Moffat stressed the opportunities presented to teachers in upgrading their qualifications within the district. That came courtesy of the UBC extension courses, but also with the promise of a

---

[79] Minutes of School Board Regular Meeting, 8 November 1965.

[80] The program with UBC was offered as long as Professor Ron Baker was willing to live here. In 1964, it became difficult to find a UBC professor willing to become resident here. None appeared to want to leave Vancouver for extended periods and with UBC's strong growth, there were no professors available. At that point, School District No. 57 withdrew from the UBC program. Harold explains that the reason for giving up on UBC, after operating successfully for four years, was the contrast with Simon Fraser University. He describes their approach as being more flexible and aggressive in setting up programs.

community college about to be built. In 1962, the province published the MacDonald Report on Higher Education which recommended that four colleges be established in the province at Prince George, in the South Cariboo, in the Kootenays and in the Okanagan. The next year, a Regional College Committee was formed, and that began the steady progress towards the institution which was given the name "College of New Caledonia" in 1963, honouring the name given to the area by explorer Simon Fraser.

In recognition of his constant and determined support for creating a college, when the province created the first governing council in November 1967, Harold Moffat was prominent among the list of government appointees. Chaired by Sam Evans (an engineer), the other government appointees were Al Mooney (a physician) and A.J. McDougal (a mine manager). They served with five others appointed by the School Board.

Chapter VI

Community Service and Sixties'Activism in Prince George

Applying the perspective of a long-time businessman to his sense of civic duty, Harold Moffat actively participated in building this city.

He's taken on leadership roles in business organizations, on the school board, and from the Mayor's chair. If there is a resident expert on how Prince George has changed over the years, that would be found in Harold Moffat.

As one indication of his impact on the city of Prince George, consider what all is packed into a two paragraph summary from a speech delivered by media personality and commentator Bob Harkins in 1999:

> During his term as Mayor, he brought the Canfor pulp mills and the oil refinery into the City tax base. He was the Mayor when the Barrett government came into power in BC and Municipal Affairs Minister Jim Lorimer decreed that Prince George would amalgamate with its outlying areas. A referendum was held in 1975 to determine if South Fort George, the Hart Highway, North Nechako, College Heights, Haldi Road, Western Acres and Blackburn would join the City. It passed by a very slim margin and in one giant gulp – 63

thousand acres were absorbed by the city, increasing its size five-fold.[81]

During Moffat's administration, the Downtown Parking Commission was formed and the first downtown parkade was built. Mayor Moffat vigorously opposed the building of the present Library but was outvoted by the majority of his Council. He fought the Kelfor Pine Centre development and lost. He spearheaded the Plaza 400 development and won. His administration purchased residents' homes in the Cache and moved most of the Cache dwellers to other areas of the City, clearing the way for extensive park and recreational development in the area.[82]

The Prince George Hockey Club met in November 1942 to plan the season. The first order of business that evening in the Prince George Hotel was electing Harold "HAM" Moffat as president to succeed Dr. Ewert who stayed on as a director along with Harold's father, A.B. Moffat, Harry Thacker, T.A. Griffith and the team captains. The goal was to field four teams – two from the Army, one from Carter-Halle-A. Kinger Co. Ltd., and one from the city – to make up the league.

---

[81] This was the eleventh boundary expansion since the city's incorporation.
[82] Excerpt from a speech by Bob Harkins to the Forum 2000 Millennium Series event, 7 October 1999.

During the fall of 1943, the Prince George Junior Chamber of Commerce elected Harold Moffat as President, moving up from the Vice-President position he'd held previously. Their first fundraising effort was purchase of a suction inhalator for the city hospital. Harold continued to serve on the executive until the end of March in 1945, when he resigned as a director.

The next month, the first Ratepayers' association in Prince George formed in November 1943. They also elected Harold Moffat as President. At that meeting, their stated aim was explained by Dr. Alward as:

> The primary purpose of a Ratepayers' association is to see that civic money is spent wisely and one dollar value is received for every dollar provided by ratepayers.[83]

One of the longest commitments to any volunteer body was his legendary 23 years' service as a member of the School Board. There were a few stints as Chairman, (first in 1945 and again in 1951 and 1956) which necessitated trips to Vancouver and Victoria, but for most of those years, he was a regular member who never missed a meeting. The few absences recorded represent times when he was away from the city.

---

[83] "Ratepayers Form Association and Elect Provisional Officers," Prince George Citizen, 2 December 1943. Dr. Alward had been promoted as president but had to decline because he was not a property owner.

A singular honour came to Harold Moffat in 1967. That was the decision of the Rotary Club of Prince George to bestow upon him the title Citizen of the Year. The award was made July 1, 1967 and is recorded on a distinctive plaque reading:

> The Rotary Club of Prince George is pleased and privileged to honour and pay tribute to
> Harold A. Moffat
> in recognition of his many and valued contributions to the welfare of this community.
> In token thereof, we hereby pronounce him to be named Citizen of the Year.

Industrial Development Commission

In the early 1960s, Harold Moffat chaired the Prince George and District Industrial Development Commission. That organization, comprised of the Mayor and an alderman; three representatives of the Chamber; and four industry members representing BC Hydro, Inland Natural Gas, and the agriculture and forestry sectors met to investigate the means to attract the industries desirable to the city's growth and development.

In his report for 1962, Harold highlighted the studies undertaken that year. They included a study on agricultural development potential of combined tree and agricultural farming; a brief on forestry presented to the legislature and another presented to the pulp mill hearing.

The group encouraged establishment of a manufacturing plant; lobbied the federal government for more favourable freight rates and for installation of an instrument landing system at the airport. They actively pursued establishment of various industries including a chemical plant, a refinery, a second pulp mill, a plywood plant and other related enterprises.

Some successes were realized immediately; others took years to come about. That economic development is a slow process with unpredictable outcomes was expressed in a fitting allegory. As an avid horseman, he related:

> You may recall that last year I commented that the work of the Industrial Development Commission is much like my experience in raising race horses. Not every year do you get the mare to foal. This year, I am pleased to report, the mare is in foal – which proves that it pays to keep on trying.[84]

Promotion:

All business ventures require attention to marketing if they're to be successful. That fact was not lost on the Industrial Development Commission which sought to raise the city's profile in some imaginative ways.

---

[84] Minutes of the Prince George & District Industrial Development Commission, 12 January 1963, p. 2.

Among the first of the promotional gimmicks developed was an idea generated by Harold and Ken Mackenzie, who was a partner in Prince George Printers. For conventioneers, he made up name plates out of thin plywood which sported a photograph of Prince George in the background. All the "vital statistics" concerning the city were printed on the back. The idea was to slip the wooden name plate into the breast pocket for the duration of a convention. They were also given to visiting dignitaries. Later on, similar buttons were made for Rotary – so the idea did have some longevity.

When the Grey Cup was held for the first time in Vancouver in 1958, the Industrial Development Commission ensured there was a Prince George presence in the Grey Cup Parade. Chuck Ewart had a float made – a platform which towed the wooden statue of Mr. PG. Bill Jones, the engineer at City Hall, perfected the float's mechanisms. Harold Moffat and Chuck Ewart took bags of Spruce Dollars and walked along the parade route distributing them to the crowds lining the streets.

Spruce Dollars were also provided to some Prince George merchants to give away to visitors. Turned out by Elroy Garden, the "dollar" was a little bit chunky in that it was "minted" a quarter inch thick with a 3-inch diameter. It bore a map of British Columbia with a hole drilled in the centre marking Prince George at the intersection of the major highways and the two railways. Around the perimeter were the words: "The

Centre City of British Columbia. The Western White Spruce Capital of the World." On the obverse, there appeared the explanation that the item was One Spruce Dollar ($1.00) commemorating the 1958 Grey Cup Parade. There were also instructions about its use: "Negotiable only for merchandise by visitors to the White Spruce Capital. One per visitor."

Although not all merchants were thrilled about accepting the Spruce Dollar, it had its appeal to people outside Prince George. While serving as Mayor, Harold recalled taking Premier W.A.C. Bennett to the airport. He had the opportunity to present him with one. "He was impressed with our Spruce Dollars."[85] The premier especially liked the innovative way of demonstrating that Prince George was the geographic centre of the province. Eventually, somebody informed Harold that a few years later a numismatic society valued that "currency" at $4.00 each.

Once again, this type of promotional technique was tried with the Pulp Bill. The first ones were for John Morrison (who served as the City's Mayor in 1956 and 1957) when he was made 1965-1966 District Governor for Rotary. Printed in green ink on a stiff piece of pulp about the size of a dollar bill, the Prince George Pulp Bill featured a photograph of District Governor Morrison inside the Rotary International wheel in the place where the Queen's portrait normally appeared.

---

[85] Interview with Harold Moffat, 1 February 1996.

The face of the bill read "Prince George Pulp Bill – A Product of Our North Woods – 52nd Annual Conference District 504 – 1966 – The Home of PULP, POWER and PEOPLE, Prince George, Canada.   Guaranteed by the Bank of Rotary." On the obverse was Rotary's Four-Way Test of the things we think, say or do: "1. Is it the TRUTH?; 2. Is it FAIR to all concerned?; 3. Will it build GOOD WILL and BETTER FRIENDSHIPS?; 4. Will it be BENEFICIAL to all concerned?"

Despite being an attractive souvenir, it didn't catch on the same way as the Spruce Dollar did.

Pulp Industry:

During the 1950s, the Prince George City Council had seen the possibility of generating revenue from the chip resource. Peter Bentley came to town and talked to the Council about that potential.   For $600 Larry De Grace produced a feasibility study which showed we had enough for a thousand ton pulp mill. An additional attraction was that Prince George's pine and spruce chips are renowned for making better, whiter pulp.

Before the pulp mills established in the 1960s, the idea promoted to create revenue from sawmill scraps was to send the chips to Vancouver rather than send it up in smoke. Eventually, Jack Pine got used in pulpmaking. That tree was once considered a weed but eventually became the backbone of pulp and paper production in this country.

Fortunes began to turn around for the city in rapid order. Harold recounted the chain of events:

> Noranda came in. We had a meeting with them. Adam Zimmerman came, too. Noranda bought out Sinclair Spruce, which was the beginning of Northwood. Northwood bought into MacBlo after that.[86]

Prince George is now recognized as the pulp capital of the world. There are six large pulp mills located within 100 miles of Prince George, counting those in Quesnel and Mackenzie.

Another idea promoted then, expanding on the wood industry, was to have more value-added products manufactured in Prince George. Despite a few starts, furniture building and specialty wood products just didn't work. Harold acknowledged the major problem: There was no way that companies could compete with child labour in the Third World.

Mining

Harold was among those Prince George leaders who pushed to have the railway put through to Fort St. James, hoping it would open up mineral claims.

---

[86] Interview with Harold Moffat, 14 November 1995.

Since then, he's become an advocate that a mine's size should be equated with the years of production. Not just 10 or 20 years, which doesn't give people who invested in homes a chance to clear themselves of mortgage debt. Citing the example of a mine in the Babine country, he claims that should not have been shut down and argues that it would have been better to let the town live on. But, there wasn't any other mineralized area around here.

The finest clay in the world is located here, eleven different varieties. But, there is not enough local market demand to support a manufacturing industry. A factor holding back production is that it is actually cheaper to take the clay out where labour is not expensive and have the product sold elsewhere. Freight rates are another stumbling block.

Support for the College of New Caledonia

CNC grew from modest beginnings in an old portable building set up beside the new Prince George Secondary School in the summer of 1968. That school was the finest and most up-to-date high school built between 1954 and 1956.

When the new high school was being planned, the city needed an assembly hall, which is how Vanier Hall got put in place. The government gave assistance but the auditorium space had to be "designed" as a four-class classroom. Other driving factors were the need for a library, with the thought that a school so equipped could become a centre for higher learning.

Attempts were also made to get second year university into the high school. At the time, students were getting into mechanical and trades training, so a vocational facility was put in place to accommodate that interest.

CNC moved into rooms in the high school to offer its first classes. The college didn't yet have approval to build, so the planners lobbied support by putting out a newspaper about the advantages a college would bring to the community. A referendum was held, but it was lost, and for days afterwards, everybody was in gloom. That event firmed up resolve in Harold Moffat to run for Mayor and take on a prominent leadership role in establishing a permanent site for the college.

The first Principal was Wolfgang Franke. Harold recalls him as difficult to work with – knowledgeable – but with an aggravating habit of threatening to quit if he didn't get his way. That tactic got suspended after the founding board informed him it was tiresome and wouldn't work. He quit in February 1970 shortly after the college began and returned to Ontario.

Then began a search for another principal to head the college. Dr. Fred Speckeen was appointed, arriving in June 1970 to an institution comprised of a staff of 31 and a student population of about 400. Dr. Speckeen said he didn't need a fancy building, just good lighting.   (He was an electrician!)   Harold observed that he went through the difficult time of amalgamating together laymen and academic staff.

Centrum Plan of 1967

Determined to see some improvement and planning for downtown development, Harold was determined to find the means to commission a study concerning the best way to proceed in the downtown core.

He canvassed the business people in the downtown area and raised $30,000 from them in one afternoon. The downtown merchants bore the cost through a levy set by Harold Moffat according to the width of store frontages. Prince George architect, Des Parker, was commissioned to produce the architectural drawings.   Once ready, the document was named "The Centrum Plan."   With some fanfare, the Downtown Businessmen's Association unveiled the ideas for developing the city's business area.

Hailed as progressive and futuristic, the plan called for high rise parkades close to shopping streets; roofs over Third Avenue, Quebec and George Streets, apartment blocks and a monorail. The CNR station was the main core with other transportation modes – a bus station and a monorail – connecting to it. Canopies were to go up and be extended to form a bridge across the street. Third Avenue would then be closed, and a ground-floor mall, with some second story retail space would be created.

With lack of political will to bring the plan into being, and the beginning of development outside the downtown core, it became a dream. The ambition expressed in the Centrum Plan is now housed on a shelf at City Hall.

Once Harold became Mayor in 1970, he championed extending the canopies down Third Avenue. Canopies were already in place at Third Avenue and Victoria. Steel canopies were erected in front of the Northern. They are structurally strong enough to hold a second story, and could help form a bridge across the street or a platform for the monorail which was proposed at the time. The rest of the canopies along Third Avenue got installed using funding from the provincial government in celebration of the province's Centennial in 1971. Shortly after that, the rest of the plan stalled. In those years, there was no city planning department, and therefore leadership to carry forward was lacking.

He encouraged council to support spending $25,500 to improve Third Avenue. The cost was to cover conversion to a one-way street to facilitate movement in and out of the parking spaces, and installation of ornamental lighting and planter boxes.

Alderman Carrie Jane Gray (who had been Mayor in 1958 and 1959) objected and became quite vocal in her accusations that the improvements were exclusively for the benefit of the business owners. It was a small spat, but it portended what was to come. She became

Mayor Moffat's main sparring partner. Some of their exchanges became legendary.

The Centrum Plan got abandoned with the coming of the Pine Centre Mall. "I could have squashed it. There were not enough aldermen to pass that development. But, I let it go. The malls are going to kill themselves, though, because there is not enough business."[87]

Harold believes there is no hope now for the Centrum Plan because of so many factions. Shop owners are too diverse and there are absentee owners of many downtown buildings. In the original Centrum Plan, two blocks were planned to become a big shopping centre with rebuilding along Third Avenue. A large group, Cadillac Fairview, was going to develop it. Harold said if it went ahead, the Northern wouldn't have been able to afford the rent to stay there. The plan was to pay according to the store frontage.

Support had been strong, but the will to proceed had not been strong enough. There were others who let it be known later on of their interest. Paddy Moran, who owned the Connaught Hotel further down on Third Avenue (on land the Courthouse now occupies) felt left out. He said, "Why didn't you come and see me? I'm interested in this town!"[88]

On Taking Action:

---

[87] Interview with Harold Moffat, 14 November 1995.
[88] Recounted in an interview with Harold Moffat 20 February 1997. Paddy Moran served also as a magistrate.

A man who speaks his mind and keeps a practical perspective cannot be constrained by niceties, arbitrariness or capricious decision-making. That was the approach Harold Moffat brought to city administration and, generally, the way he does business. The focus has always been on getting things accomplished. Sometimes that meant placing more emphasis on action than serving bureaucracy or process.

One outstanding example occurred during his first year in office as Mayor when serious flooding threatened the homes of people living on Cottonwood Island. At one point, the water rose eight inches in fifteen minutes, and evacuations were necessary. After that began a long process of determining the value of the homes, paying compensation and relocating all the residents. Extensive files include photographs which reveal that most of the homes were small shacks. Still, they were home to the families living there and most wanted to stay. Relocating everyone became a long, drawn-out process.

Hazel Huckvale, a pioneer teacher and long-time resident of this region knew Harold through their school board involvement. She was delighted that he became Mayor and approved of the changes he brought about in the 1970s. "I think Harold Moffat was a gift to Prince George. The city needed him to bring it along and become a more developed place."[89]

---

[89] Interview with Hazel Huckvale, 23 May 1998.

A development which has benefitted generations of sports enthusiasts is creation of the Prince George Golf & Curling Club. Harold was a founding member when the club was revived after the war in 1945. Until a clubhouse was built, meetings were held at city hall.

During the 1940s, Harold golfed regularly every Thursday with Bob Madill, Jimmy Wilson and Ivor Killy. If ever one of their foursome couldn't make it, somebody would be recruited to make up the group. One day, a new young fellow was approached. He asked "What do you play for?" and was told "five, five and five." They found out later that he'd been concerned that he couldn't afford the $5.00 for the round but was relieved when each started putting up a nickel. The "pot" was used to buy pop and chocolate bars at the end of the game.

There was also interest in the welfare of the region and province. For a period during the years Robert Bonner served as Chairman of BC Hydro (1976 to 1985), Harold Moffat was appointed to the BC Hydro board. Together with a few other board members, Harold started looking at that crown corporation's financial policies. After that sub-committee put forward recommendations for cost-savings, then Minister of Energy, Mines and Petroleum Resources, Stephen Rogers, fired them from the board and replaced them with Vancouver-based appointees. That action angered Harold.

To this day, Harold Moffat is engaged with and interested in the life of this city. The back counter at The Northern is still a place where significant events of the day are discussed and advice freely given.

GOLF IN QUESNEL

When the mood strikes him, he commits thoughts and suggestions to paper and shares them with politicians who might benefit from his experience.

After all, there aren't many issues which he hasn't encountered and thought through many times before.

Chapter VII

In The Mayor's Chair

The City Hall Years – 1970 to 1978

1970

Harold Moffat came to run for the Mayor's job while he was serving as a member of the governing council at the College of New Caledonia. Seeing the Aldermen and Mayor vote down the proposal for the college inspired him to vie for the city's top job. He had strong convictions that there needed to be ongoing education for those students not going to university but had interest in studying for a vocation.

Mayor Garvin Dezell stepped down, deciding not to run in the fall 1969 election. That opened a chance to run. He had wanted one of his aldermen to declare, and Hilliard Clare volunteered. Ten days later, Harold Moffat declared and they had a friendly, short campaign. It was comprised of a few civic meetings at the Simon Fraser Hotel and a session with the Junior Chamber of Commerce.

Hilliard Clare happened to be Harold's friend, a longtime employee of The Northern, and an Alderman on Mayor Dezell's Council since 1960. Many people in Prince George were torn about the vote that year, since both men were well known and had many friends in common. The outcome was that Harold Moffat was elected Mayor with six aldermen: Elroy Garden, Carrie-Jane Gray[90], Jack Heinrich, Harry Loder, Lorne McCuish, and Alfred Nunweiler. Harold showed up at Hilliard's "losing" party. It was just a short walk because they were neighbours on Laurier Crescent.

It was on January 5th, 1970 at the regular Council meeting held at noon that Harold Moffat's term as Mayor began. On that day, he swore the Mayor's Oath of Office:

I, HAROLD ALEXANDER MOFFAT, Mayor Elect for the City of Prince George, do declare that I am a British Subject, possessing the qualifications by law required, and that I am not in any way disqualified from holding the office of Mayor and I have not, nor will have while holding the office, any interest directly or indirectly, in any contract or services connected with the Corporation except such as I may lawfully have under the provisions of the Municipal Act in that behalf, I have not by myself, or by any other persons, knowingly employed any bribery, corruption or intimidation to gain my election and I will faithfully perform the

---

[90] Carrie-Jane Gray served as Mayor in 1958 and 1959 and as Alderman from 1964 to 1977, when she retired. When she ran for Mayor, A.B. Moffat signed her nomination papers.

duties of my office and will not allow any private interest to influence my conduct in public matters.

Signed H.A. Moffat

and immediately following, he took the Mayor's Oath of Allegiance:

I, HAROLD ALEXANDER MOFFAT, do solemnly promise and swear that I will be faithful and bear true allegiance to Her Majesty Queen Elizabeth II, her heirs and successors, So Help Me God.

Signed H.A. Moffat

In his inaugural address to Council, Mayor Moffat gave some indications of how he planned to operate. Anticipating an interesting year ahead, he suggested a schedule which would see the agenda for the weekly meetings prepared by Friday evening. Monday morning's Council meeting would be open to the public and afternoon sessions were proposed as a time for discussion within committees. As for the focus of the work, the new Mayor was definitive and specific:

I must at this time give you my thoughts on the office of Mayor and Aldermen. I feel that we are firstly makers of policy for the guidance of our administrative officers. As we must have all the facts equally and without prejudice, I would suggest that it will do no one any good to solicit or cajole any one of us. I would further suggest that problems of individuals or companies should not become problems of Council or Council members until they have proceeded though the responsible administrative departments. I would suggest too that it be desirable that as much as possible be in letter form.

We should sit as a court, hearing all evidence, and deciding whether we uphold or redesign our policy.

In the matter of public appearances, I would like to state the position I would like you to consider. I feel that much too often we are called upon to represent the City out of protocol, out of custom or for the sake of dignity. It is my feeling that one sacrifices enough of one's time on committee and City business without having to perform for the above reasons. I would suggest that we are available whenever we have a material function to perform. The material function we can define in our discussions.

In announcing the appointments to the various committees, I have done so with the aim of spreading the load as equally as possible and with as little disruption to the various departments as possible.

From time to time I will ask you to head special committees of interested citizens to study such matters as pollution, youth, environment, welfare and any other matters where I feel we need guidance.[91]

———————

This was the roster of appointments to civic committees:

REGIONAL DISTRICT	Alderman Loder
	Alderman Gray
	Mayor Moffat (alt.)
REGIONAL HOSPITAL	Alderman McCuish
CIVIC PROPERTIES	Alderman McCuish
ADVISORY PLANNING COMM.	Alderman Nunweiler
LIBRARY BOARD	Alderman Heinrich
INDUSTRIAL DEVELOPMENT COMM.	Alderman Loder
NORTHERN INTERIOR HEALTH UNIT	Alderman Gray
	Alderman Garden
CITIZENSHIP	Alderman Gray
EXHIBITION BOARD	Alderman Nunweiler
DOWNTOWN PARKING COMM.	Alderman Loder
CIVIL DEFENCE	Alderman Nunweiler
SCHOOL BOARD LIAISON COMM.	Alderman Heinrich (Chair)
	Alderman Garden
	Alderman McCuish
	Mayor Moffat
FINANCE	Alderman Garden (Chair)
	Alderman Heinrich
	Mayor Moffat
COMMUNITY DEVELOPMENT COMM.	Alderman McCuish (Chair)

———————————————

[91] Excerpt from the Mayor's inaugural address, appended to the minutes of the regular Council meeting, 5 January 1970.

Mr. B. Scholton

Mr. P. Baker

Mr. A. Thomson

Mayor H. Moffat

Mr. J. Ter Heide

BOARD OF VARIANCE Mr. H. Clare

YELLOWHEAD HIGHWAY ASSOC. Mr. Garvin Dezell

FAMILY COURT Alderman Gray

Being Mayor was not then a full-time job. The work of governing the city was conducted according to meetings scheduled by the Mayor's office or for special ceremonial events. Harold went to work at The Northern in the morning, and then to city hall in the afternoon, as needed.

With an eye to cost-savings for the City, Mayor Moffat announced a decision on Thursday, January 7th that henceforth, snow would not be removed from residential streets on weekends. He also put a stop to the cost of renting extra snow removal equipment and paying crews overtime for that purpose. As luck would have it, the very next day one of the biggest dumps of snow hit the city. It was so overwhelming, city engineer Ernie Obst had to order a midnight shift to clear the downtown area. Nothing happened in residential areas, following the Mayor's announced change in policy. As a result, city hall was overwhelmed with complaint calls from those snowed in, particularly in the sub-divisions.

At the Monday night council meeting, Alderman Carrie-Jane Gray spoke out criticizing

the Mayor for "his penny-pinching attitude."
She continued with the point that it was
"absolutely ridiculous that in these times people
should be forced to wallow through knee-deep
snow." Alderman Elroy Garden was also in
opposition and proposed "that our standards of
snow removal not be changed." His motion was
supported by Aldermen Lorne McCuish, Alf
Nunweiler and Carrie-Jane Gray. The only one
who sided with Mayor Moffat was Alderman Jack
Heinrich who believed that there should be
attempts to keep snow removal costs in check.[92]

The result of the 4-1 vote was a return to
the previous policy of opening arterial routes,
bus routes, residential collector streets and then
to clear all the residential streets. Mayor Moffat
stated that he believed it could still be possible
to contain costs. He acknowledged that the city
was bound by a union agreement to pay crews
overtime for any work performed on weekends.
In an editorial published a few days later,
comment was put forward that this idea worked
in Red Deer where even worse snow conditions
prevailed (up to 30 inch snowfalls). The editor
commented that those Albertans   must be
"endowed with an unusual amount of
forbearance" and concluded "Mayor Moffat can
hardly be blamed for trying."[93]

---

[92] For 1970, the city budget allowed $72,000 for snow removal;
$43,000 for sanding and $36,000 for plowing. As a prank, Chuck
Ewart plastered City signs and stickers all over his own front-end
loader and ceremoniously plowed only the Mayor's driveway.

[93] Prince George Citizen editorial, written by editor A.N. (Tony) Skae
published 15 January 1970, p. 2.

Civic asset

You don't necessarily have to be a railway buff to appreciate city council's decision to allocate funds for the construction of a miniature railway in Fort George Park.

It helps though, if you have a sense of history and a modicum of civic pride.

The engine that will pull the proposed train and which was lovingly restored by Mr. Thomas McLennan, was, if our history is correct, the first work train to pull into Prince George when the Grand Trunk Pacific arrived in 1914. For many years the "dinky" engine graced a small park on CN property at the foot of George St. before it was turned over to the Fort George Museum Society for restoration.

The city proposes to apply for a charter to operate the railway and according to Ald. Bob Martin, an enthusiastic proponent, a budget of $16,000 will provide the line with a station and engine house within the Fort George Museum compound as well as about half a mile of track.

If it is half as successful as Vancouver's Stanley Park railway, the city's investment will be returned with interest.

If such is the case, no small measure of credit must go to the city's works superintendent, the innovative Bill Jones, who has been working on the project for several years and to others like Mayor Harold Moffat who was there with cash out of his own pocket to ensure the restoration of the locomotive.

MINIATURE RAILWAY IN FORT GEORGE PARK

The pulp mill development of the previous decade had caused the population to increase by 10,000 people over that period. In 1970, Prince George was home to 35,000 people, and began attracting the attention of national media. One reporter visiting from Montreal got Mayor Moffat to describe his approach to running the city, thereby recording one of the best and most candid insights into the "let's get on with it" attitude that prevailed:

> "I don't even look at the Municipal Act unless I think it might do something for me," said Mayor Harold Moffat, hardware merchant." "If it's going to hamper me, I don't want to know about it until after I've done what I'm going to do. I fly by the seat of my pants and I think that is possibly the attitude we should develop in Canada....You get into a lot of theory and bickering and meanwhile years are going by and we're not accomplishing what we should be."[94]

At a June meeting, the Council turned attention to the issue of a property reserve for an anticipated building of a university some time in the future. Aldermen Jack Heinrich and Elroy Garden proposed that Council concur with the Committee recommendation: "That the Minister of Lands, Forest and Water Resources be petitioned to make certain that the University Site area on the top of Cranbrook Hill is not in any way alienated from the Crown's ownership."[95]

---

[94] Joseph MacSween, Canadian Press article, published in The Prince George Citizen, 3 June 1970, p. 10.
[95] Minutes of Regular Council Meeting, 1 June 1970.

Mr.PG

During the first regular Council meeting in July, Alderman Carrie-Jane Gray had information she wished to share under New Business. She advised Council that she was receiving complaints about the lack of appointment of ladies to the various commissions. She announced "His Worship advised that while he was Mayor he would make no appointments of women to the various commissions." This became a sticking point with her, although women had served on Council committees in prior years.

Thinking back on that battle with Alderman Gray, Harold recalls that it was his thinking that as women spent less time in the home with their families, there were more problems with society.[96] He began to equate women's involvement in full-time employment with the downfall of society. This recognized that the time commitment to serving on committees and commissions was enormous. On this subject, there never was a meeting of minds. "She and I fought for years. At almost every Council meeting she'd come up with something contentious."[97]

During October, a series of events began to unfold in Quebec which threatened the security and stability familiar in Canadian society. What was later referred to as "the October Crisis" was precipitated by the actions of the Front de Liberation du Quebec (FLQ) which kidnapped British Trade Commissioner James Cross and Quebec Justice Minister Pierre Laporte. The FLQ's agenda was to promote an independent and socialist Quebec. Escalation of violence and threats to the lives of innocent people raised alarm across the country.

---

[96] Interview with Harold Moffat, 9 February 1997.
[97] Ibid.

The federal government acted to invoke the War Measures Act, which resulted in a temporary suspension of civil liberties. On Friday, October 16, Prime Minister Pierre Trudeau addressed the nation. Part of his address included:

> I am speaking to you at a moment of grave crisis, when violent and fanatical men are attempting to destroy the unity and the freedom of Canada.
>
> ...
>
> If a democratic society is to continue to exist, it must be able to root out the cancer of an armed, revolutionary movement that is bent on destroying the very basis of our freedom. For that reason, the Government, following an analysis of the facts, including requests of the Government of Quebec and the City of Montreal for urgent action, decided to proclaim the War Measures Act. It did so at 4:00 a.m. this morning, in order to permit the full weight of Government to be brought quickly to bear on all those persons advocating or practising violence as a means of achieving political ends.
>
> ...
>
> The Government is acting as well to ensure the safe return of Mr. James Cross and Mr. Pierre Laporte. I speak for millions of Canadians when I say to

their courageous wives and families how much we sympathize with them for the nightmare to which they have been subjected, and how much we all hope and pray that it will soon conclude.[98]

Canadians were sickened by the news report the next day that Pierre Laporte had been murdered. The gravity of the national crisis affected sensibilities everywhere. As the Prince George City Council met on October 19, Aldermen Carrie-Jane Gray and Elroy Garden proposed that Council concur with Mayor Moffat's message sent to the Prime Minister through Bob Borrie, the Member of Parliament for the riding of Prince George—Peace River:

Mr. Prime Minister:

I feel that I speak for the vast majority of the people of Prince George when I congratulate you and the Government of Canada for the measures you have invoked to suppress lawlessness in Canada.

May I suggest that all here would agree that there should be no relaxation of the Government's policy.

---

[98] Pierre Elliott Trudeau, notes for a national broadcast, October 16, 1970. Pierre Laporte's body was discovered the next day. James Cross was released December 3rd following discovery by the police of the place he was being held. Ultimately, the kidnappers were exiled to Cuba, but all eventually returned to Canada.

And also that a further message be sent to Laporte's family on behalf of the Citizens of Prince George.

The Council put on record unanimous support for that message. Looking back on that communication, Harold commented on the reason for communicating with the Prime Minister: "To let the Prime Minister know that we wanted law and order to prevail in Canada."[99] The crisis was not considered to have passed until troops withdrew from Quebec on Christmas Eve 1970.

By November, City Council was concentrating again on local concerns. At issue was where the statue of Mr. Pee Gee should be located. Some believed that it should go in front of the Chamber of Commerce office at 15th and Victoria. However, at the November 16th meeting, Aldermen Lorne McCuish and Elroy Garden proposed that $500 of contingency expense money be used to move the statue to the intersection of Highways 16 and 97 adjacent to the Tourist Bureau.

1971

Council's first meeting for the year was held January 4. At that time, Mayor Moffat opened by declaring "I would like to express my appreciation to the Council of 1970 for their forbearance and dedication during my first year in office."[100]   He extended remarks of

---

[99] Interview with Harold Moffat, 9 February 1997.
[100] Minutes of Regular Council Meeting, 4 January 1971.

appreciation for former Alderman Harry Loder who had been appointed to chair the planning committee for the province's Centennial celebrations. In his place, Joe Ter Heide had been elected Alderman.

Looking to the year ahead, the Mayor's agenda included fulfillment of some plans and the continuation or commencement of others. He provided a list of priorities as:

> low income housing project
> installation of canopies over sidewalks on Third Avenue and George Street
> subdivision expansion program
> public safety building
> projects for cultural and recreational development
> sewage treatment program
> new waterworks intake station
> planning for projected boundary expansion

Despite his pronouncement the year before that he would not appoint women to any boards or commissions, the names of Miss Valerie Kordyban and Mrs. Jose Smith appear as members of the Centennial '71 Committee; Monica Williams and Arlene Gray to the Family Court Committee; and Daphne Baldwin, Winnifred Murphy and Phyllis Parker to the Library Commission.

Supported by Lorne McCuish and Alf Nunweiler, Council considered and passed a motion at the February 15th meeting recommending that the city proceed with building a new police facility on city-owned property at the corner of Tenth Avenue and Brunswick Street. The reported cost of construction was estimated at $954,172[101]. The building's design was created by Prince George architect, Des Parker.

Prince George started to anticipate the May 10th visit of Queen Elizabeth II as part of the royal tour in celebration of the province's Centennial year. By the beginning of April, the parade route had been established which would take Her Majesty along Patricia Avenue to Gorse to the north entrance of Fort George Park with a tour through the park's northern area and introduction to visiting mayors of the region. A lot of preparation, including some dry runs of the route and ceremony, went into planning for the Queen's hour-long visit. Amid all the frenzied arrangements, a telephone call came to Harold at home one evening around 7:00 p.m. It was a man with a pronounced English accent who had all kinds of improbable questions about the security arrangements and the expectations Scotland Yard had for the Queen's protection. After a few exasperating minutes, the caller finally identified himself as Harold's friend – a

---

[101] Minutes of Special Council Meeting, 1 September 1971, reflected that the tender was won by the lowest bidder, Narod Construction Company, for $809,015. Two days later, the company informed the city by telegram, read to the city manager at 4:45 p.m. that, due to a mathematical error in their submission, Narod wished to withdraw their tender. On September 7th, the contract was awarded to the second lowest bidder, Parkins Construction, for $836,800. The city then sued Narod for the difference of $27,785.

mischievous practical joker – none other than Chuck B. Ewart.

While here, Her Majesty happened to ask Mayor Moffat about the city's name change from Fort George to Prince George. In a report prepared a few days later, he stated, "I would ask the Citizen to dig out of their files the history of the name change from Fort George to Prince George. I was embarrassed not to answer the Queen's question more authoritatively."[102]

---

[102] Mayor's Report, 13 May 1971. When the city of Prince George was incorporated on March 6, 1915, there was controversy over whether to keep the name as "Fort" or change to "Prince" which was regarded as a more progressive-sounding name. The issue was settled with a plebiscite held at the inaugural election May 20, 1915. The result was that 153 voters wanted "Prince George" to just 13 wishing to keep it as "Fort George". The name honours England's Prince George who was then 13 years old. He was the fourth son (and fifth child) of King George V and Princess Victoria Mary.

A proclamation prepared by the province's Attorney-General effected the name change. It read:

"GEORGE the FIFTH, by the Grace of God, of the United Kingdom of Great Britain and Ireland, and of the British Dominions beyond the Seas, King, Defender of the Faith, Emperor of India.

GREETING. A PROCLAMATION.

NOW KNOW YE that by virtue of the authority contained in Section 12 of the "Fort George Incorporation Act," We do hereby order and proclaim that on, from and after the publication of this proclamation in two consecutive issues of the British Columbia Gazette, the municipality incorporated under the name "City of Fort George" by Chapter 29 of the Statutes of British Columbia, 1915, shall be known by the name "City of Prince George."

Later, Prince George became the Duke of Kent. He saw active service during the Second World War and died while on duty. In August 1942, his plane crashed into a hillside in Scotland.

CITY PIONEER RALPH NEHRING

Two far-reaching decisions formed the Mayor's report in May. One was direction to the engineering department to go ahead with preparing plans to call for tenders on the erection of canopies over the sidewalks on Third Avenue and George Street. The other was consideration for naming the new subdivision.

Mayor Moffat expressed his preference that it be named "Heritage Park" to align with the decision to name its streets after City pioneers. Until then, the proposal had been to call it "Centennial" (reflecting the fact that 1971 was British Columbia's centennial year) and the Mayor's concern was that farther into the future, people would not be aware of which centennial that honoured.

To that point, streets had been named using an ABCD system, then river and lake names. The subdivision was named "Heritage" and the Mayor's list of old-timers was used for street names.

In one of the first controversial decisions, Mayor Moffat voted against the rest of Council in July for the expenditure of monies for renovations to the Library.[103] He didn't see it as a community resource or a centre of activity for residents. Plain and simple, a library was just a place to warehouse books. At the time, computers were becoming used primarily for record and data storage. To Harold's way of thinking, information would end up being stored that way. Thinking back to that stand, he commented "I think I'll be proven right. Books will be delivered on the computer. If an old

---

[103] Minutes of Regular Council Meeting 12 July 1971. A discussion was entertained on the subject of proceeding with library renovations. A motion carried "That Council reaffirm the decision of May 17, 1971, with regard to the awarding of the contract for the Library renovations." It had been proposed and supported by Alf Nunweiler and Lorne McCuish, with the Mayor recording he was voting against the motion.

hardware merchant could see that, then surely librarians should."[104]

One of the biggest and most contentious issues facing Council in 1971 arose over the planning and design of the City's sewage treatment system. Dr. Vern Johnson, a local physician, took up the crusade to go to a secondary system. Until then, the solution was going to be to dry and then burn the sludge. If that had been allowed, the College Heights district would have suffered most from the smoke.

At the August 16th meeting, Council had resolved that Associated Engineering Services Ltd. be instructed to complete a design for sewer treatment facilities which would include primary treatment and incineration. After considering what that meant, and after investigating sewage treatment systems incorporated elsewhere, Mayor Moffat became convinced that there was a better approach.

The Prince George City Council had a strong sense of responsibility and concern for not polluting the Fraser River and thereby causing any hardship or health problems for neighbours downstream.

Dr. Johnson travelled with a group to Victoria to lobby against having only a primary treatment system funded. On that occasion, Mayor Moffat met an engineer, Ray Cunliffe, and became interested in having his firm, Willis,

---

[104] Interview with Harold Moffat, 9 February 1997.

Cunliffe and Tate, invited to submit an alternate proposal from the one which had been drafted by Associated Engineering Services Ltd. before Mayor Moffat took office. Interest in an alternate firm came about first because Harold believed they could do a better job, and also because, up to that point, Associated Engineers had a history of having the city as a client and virtually held a monopoly on the city's engineering problems. It occurred to the Mayor that it might be time for change.

The Mayor's research convinced him that Prince George should have a high-rate secondary system to handle sewage. He raised his concerns at the public hearing held September 7.

His objection was based in two points. His concern was over incineration of sludge and installation of only primary clarifiers. Although there had not previously been much sharing among cities, he sought and received advice about the operation of many other municipal systems. He read all of the material sent to him and from the report produced, it is evident that he had much more than a passing familiarity with the subject. Prince George was, in fact, among the first (after Quesnel) to be considering installation of a secondary treatment plant.

He produced a detailed report for Council's consideration setting out the information and the rationale behind his convictions:

MAYOR'S REPORT

Under Section 180 of the Municipal Act, I return for
reconsideration the following Resolution of Council passed
August 16, 1971:
"It was moved by Ald. Heinrich, and seconded by Ald.
Garden, that Council concur with the Committee
recommendation that Associated Engineering Service
Limited be instructed to complete the design for sewer
treatment facility with Primary Treatment and Incineration."
I return this for reconsideration upon the following reasons:
1. The Resolution is indefinite in terms of reference and
direction. From the motion, there is no direction as to what
system of Secondary Treatment is contemplated. Without
this direction, no one has authority to approve the raising
of the heights of the grit and primary sedimentation tanks
and further no one has authority to plan in the initial
installation for disposal of secondary sludge by incineration.
2. That Council has by Resolution committed itself to design
without full consideration of the design, decorum or usage
of plant buildings.
3. That Council has by Resolution committed itself to a
contract without formal documentation of that contract as
to fees, as to overages, as to guarantees.
4. I would ask that Council reconsider the Resolution in light
of a review of the evidence and new evidence that has
come to hand. However you classify the following, I feel
that I must state as evidence the reasons for my position.
The first is a fact that I feel that most of us agree on is that
we have been advised that with the volume of the Fraser
River together with its silt content, with the subsequent
rapids and canyons immediately south of our outflow, the
degree of treatment could be minimal.
Fact number two is we have been instructed by the BC
Pollution Control Board to be discharging a Primary effluent

by November 1973 and present preliminary plans of the proposed secondary by the same date.

I think most Council members thought as I did, that Primary was the initial step in sewage treatment and was a necessary step towards Secondary and then on to Tertiary. In essence, we thought the route was first by Primary removal, we acquired a 30 - 35% B.O.D.[105] product with the addition of secondary we upgraded to a possible 90% B.O.D. product with Tertiary we could accomplish a possible 98% B.O.D. product. It was on this assumption that Council commissioned A.E.S.L. to proceed with design, etc. of a primary treatment plant as a preliminary stage to a more sophisticated system.

However, it was brought to Council's attention through outside advice that there were systems available that bypass Primary and went direct to secondary. It was this that we asked for proposals from two firms on the high rate activated sludge plants. In both commissions the Degremont design plant was used as the package plant for the secondary treatment. Although the high rate plant of our capacity have not as yet been in operation in Canada, they are operating in various cities on the continent in conjunction with primary clarifiers that in all probability were installed in the initial stage when regulations were more permissive.

I agree that the primary plant that we have chosen which consists beyond the screening facility and flow meter in the existing works of a degritting chamber, a settling chamber with scrapers and sludge pumps that pick up the collectable solids and transfer them to the incinerator while all the other infected material and water with a B.O.D.

---

[105] B.O.D. (Biochemical Oxygen Demand), a common measurement in domestic sewage wastewater along with T.S.S. (Total Suspended Solids) – both of which are most desirable when kept low.

removal of 30 - 35% then proceeds through the existing Chlorinator to the outfall in the river, would meet the requirements as laid down by the Pollution Control Board by 1973. I cannot agree, however, that this permit will last for an indefinite period. What with our position as the major City on the headwaters of the Fraser, it is feasible that the strictest standards would follow downward with the river flow. With Quesnel on high rate secondary treatment regardless of whether they are discharging their sludge into the river and with the recent statements by the federal authorities and its cost sharing formula signed with Ontario, I believe we will be forced to proceed with secondary soon after the prescribed date. I think public pressure alone will compel Ottawa to adopt a similar policy in respect to secondary treatment as they did with septic tanks in the eligibility of a city for National Housing loans. In this way, they could force the independent non co-operative provinces to accept the Ottawa-Ontario agreement.

The high rate plant consists beyond the existing works of a degritting chamber, an oxy contact chamber, primary aeorbic digester that can be converted to an oxy contact tank as the population increases to 90,000 people and a secondary aerobic digester with the sludge being handled in any number of ways including incineration the water or effluent of up to 90% B.O.D. removal then goes through the existing works of chlorinator and outfall.

I realize that the Degremont proposal without primary clarifiers cannot be substantiated by working models in our design capacity, but on the other hand, I would suspect that in the beginning neither were the high rate systems substantiated by a volume working model. At some place, at some time, someone had to believe that the designers had perfected a workable idea. At this time, I would tend to believe the company that had developed through engineering and above all practical experience when they are willing to guarantee a high rate of B.O.D. removal of up to 90% from the plans they submit and do not advocate after all their experience that primary clarifiers are needed. The City of Sudbury of 84,000 population apparently is moving in this direction and a reprint from the Civic Administration, page 3 April edition advises:

Sudbury is the last city in Ontario to build a sewage treatment plant, and local taxpayers are getting a bargain. The high aeration system designed for the city bypasses the normal primary treatment stages, involving screening and settling of solids.

Consulting Engineers for the project, Underwood McLellan and Associates, believe that their design will save the City between $1 million and $2 million."

To allay any fears, I would suggest that in plant design, we allow room for primary clarifiers and also for the chemical additive tanks that research may develop. We know then that we have provided for any consequence that may arise.

In view of fact number one, we are in the most enviable position to create a possible break through in less costly sewage treatment to the secondary level. If the plant does not come up to full expectation the overall cost will be no greater than now proposed.

On sludge disposal, I think we should assess the product we are dealing with. It is my understanding that it is a practically inert material suspended in water with a 5% sludge to 95% water as it leaves the secondary digester and can be reduced by withdrawing the water by various methods and additions up to a 20% consistency. It is my understanding that the material would have no more than 5% active agents.

Therefore, my first inclination would be that if Council proceeds with a primary plant that clarifies the effluent to a 30 - 35% B.O.D. removal for discharge in the river, there should be no qualms about discharging an 80-90% B.O.D. effluent and a 5% active inert material into the river. I would think that the Pollution Control Board could have little objection to a plan that at the very minimum would raise the percentage quality of the effluent by somewhere over 100% of what they now demand.

Failing approval of this method, I would suggest that we investigate the land disposal method as practised for many years by the City of Guelph, population 51,000. From my knowledge of the soils in our area they are most suitable and are in need of any material that will loosen their tenacity. And if lime is to become a phosphate eliminator and incidentally we have local lime to cut our costs, we will have another much needed additive for the soil. We will be repeating the process of nature of putting back in the soil that which we have taken away.

Failing the practicality of liquid land disposal on farm lands, I would suggest we prepare drying beds on site for this inert material. The City Engineer's report suggests we have the acreage and have a gravel lease from which to create more.

If the bed area is needed for further expansion then maybe it is the time for incineration but nothing is wasted. The dried sludge can be lifted by front end loader. If they become overloaded, we can employ a cycling system and with our own equipment on off seasons we can schedule removal at the least possible cost. It is my feeling that sludge disposal is the larger problem of waste disposal and as such will receive the greatest amount of research activity, and I draw your attention to page 33 of the April issue of *Civic Administrator*:

"Vancouver will put its sludge to good use."

Studies into the practicality of converting sludge from treatment plants into fertilizer or soil conditioner will be carried out by the Greater Vancouver Sewerage District. The experiment will be conducted on a site adjacent to the Iona Island treatment plant. It will be carried out under the direction of Doug MacKay, the district's chief engineer. The Vancouver Park Board has expressed an interest in the project and has offered its assistance.

At present, digested sludge from the Lion's Gate plant on the North Shore is discharged to the bottom of the first narrows during periods of maximum ebb. At the Iona Island plant it is held in lagoons. At both plants the disposal of sludge has presented no problems; Iona has sufficient storage space for another 20 years or more.

But district chairman Ald. Warren Clark of Burnaby said that officials have for some time considered methods of recycling sludge. Discussions have been held with a number of groups on the possibility of using it for fertilizer or soil conditioner.

As a result, an experimental plot covering about three acres will be created on Iona Island. Cost of the experiment, including installation of irrigation equipment, is estimated at $5,000.00.

I am disturbed that in the face of all the knowledge available to the powers that be in every other city in Canada only two of them have bought the incinerator disposal method and one of these is an A.E.S.L. plant. I would suggest that if a city the size of Chicago which solved its sludge problem with a train leaving every day and going 160 miles south where it is disposed of at a rate of around two inches of liquid sludge per acre per year, and that is enough to grow a crop of corn, they certainly should investigate the relative costs of loading it into tank cars, unloading into trucks and spraying the fields against the cost of incineration. I feel that incineration should be developed hand in hand with the garbage disposal problem. This City one day will have a garbage reclaiming plant and the resultant discard material should be incinerated providing methods are found to non-pollute the air.

I do not agree with the suggestion that we will be bypassing an expensive installation if subsequent Councils decide to proceed to incineration if no new advances are made for sludge handling. I am told that the primary aerobic digester is designed to be converted to an oxy contact until when the population reaches 90,000. The secondary aerobic digester can be used as a storage unit to balance the operation of the incinerator to the convenience of the operator or as a safety valve for incinerator maintenance.

My real concern about the route we have chosen is that by incineration we are committing future Councils to a closed end operation on a subject that we have heard, read and reviewed is open ended for argument, contradiction fears and to the greatest extent is in its infancy as to research. The experiments that are going on in Ontario make me feel that we have only scratched the waste disposal problem. No one has talked to us about lime, alum, aluminum sulphate to remove phosphates, or the danger of lime and alkalinity on a combined plant for recalcinating the lime and burning the sludge. Until research reaches some basic conclusions of the best route or method to follow, then I suggest that at this time, the very best we can do is provide a high rate secondary system leaving both ends open, leaving subsequent

Councils in the position of making modifications, improving and upgrading the methods and expanding the system by on site experience and experimentation with actual costs of the experience. And above all adapting to the system the new developments that research, research and more research will uncover and in part being a party to that research.

Besides which we can employ our own resourcefulness and ingenuity to keep the operation and maintenance cost to a minimum. From what I can gather about the Degremont system, it is very simple process, with nature doing the work aided by oxygen from five large air pumps of which one is a standby unit and I see no reason why warning devices cannot be located in our fire halls. In fact it may be a good time to consider the placing of our next firehall adjacent to this site and doing away with duplicate supervision, office and staff amenities. Whereas the primary-cum-incinerator has mechanical scrapers, sludge pumps, incinerator feed systems that would be difficult to electrically engineer for warning devices.

In light of the review of old and new evidence, I would respectfully request that Council reconsider rescinding of the motion and deferring a final decision until we have time to further assess all the avenues and arguments placed before us.

Respectfully submitted, Harold A. Moffat, Mayor
September 3, 1971

The controversy over the sewage treatment decision carried on into the fall as the dominant issue in the Mayor's next report:

MAYOR'S REPORT

With or without prejudice, I think it is time that we review some of the aspects of the route to which this city is now committed and some of the fears of the Aldermen that support the route. I shall deal with the latter first but possibly not in the order of greatest concern or priority.

1. The fear of no primary clarifiers before secondary.

Let us reflect back on the Fredericton plant that set us to thinking about High rate secondary which in fact our engineers have now recommended to us for our own usage in the next stage. And whether or not you can remember if Olaf Skorzewski advised against primary before secondary, I attach a copy of the phone call I had with another member of the Degremont firm on April 21, 1971. In essence, primary upsets the uniformity of a balanced biological load to the secondary with the primary clarifiers and I would suspect even more so when you extract and burn. It would appear to me that our engineers in advocating primary clarifiers and incineration are going contrary to the advice of the supplier of this equipment and the plant design of the High rate system, namely Degremont. I therefore again request and especially in the face of the low grade of effluent we shall be discharging from the primary plant why or how one could call it a 'gamble' to directly to High rate secondary especially if plans are made for the addition of primary if necessary.

2. The fear of pollution of the land with the sludge.

a) Sludge is classified in the same category as compost only it is possibly a more refined product in as much as its incubation is more standardized.

b) For those still concerned about human contamination in the area, I would suggest they advocate the banning of horse, cow and chicken manure, or compost heaps and all dogs as they are the worst offenders. Not to mention the garbage dumps. And by no means should we allow the brand name fertilizers of Milorganic or Valganic to be used in our city because they are dried sludge.

Whether this product in a solution of 95% water, 5% sludge or less is pumped to land enrichment as planned in Edmonton or whether this product is trucked to the land in the same consistency as done in most other places and is especially recommended by the Ontario Water Resources Commission that operates the treatment centres for some 45 cities with secondary treatment or whether this product is placed on sludge drying beds for which we need three acres or an acre approximately 200 feet by 600 feet and the dried or semi-dried product is removed for burial in our sanitary land fill or is used for fertilizer or whether we take the centrifuges from the front end of the primary system now planned and use them on the back end to dehydrate the sludge to a cake consistency for burial to land fill or is used for fertilizer.

The cost factor of any of these types of disposal will be less expensive than incineration and I think they should be reviewed.

(A Complete Cost analysis was set out.)

The one pocket that will pay for a Police Building, a rink, a library expansion, a little theatre, a Centennial project plus all the added operating costs that accrue, all committed, plus in this year a new water intake system, a new trunk system for all services on our east and north undeveloped subdivisions, new fire station, to give the PGR people some return for their taxes, plus a Massey Drive Underpass, or a Cottonwood Island overpass.

There are a million places to better spend the million or more dollars than taking a chance that an air monitor on plush College Heights produces evidence to shut down the One Million Dollar over expenditure.

Food for thought.

Respectfully submitted, Harold A. Moffat, Mayor

19 November 1971

Eventually the fight came down to the opinion of a few Council members over whether or not to accept the advice of the city engineers or to take advice from outside. The issue over using just primary treatment and then pump the rest into the river or to go with a secondary treatment system split the Council. In the next election, those opposed to Harold got defeated and new aldermen came in. An engineer was hired, and his advice concurred with that of the city engineers. Harold believes that when the new aldermen came in, they made one mistake. They should have replaced the first engineering firm, but instead used them to bring in the secondary treatment plant. That system still supports the city, but it has been redesigned and revamped since.

An example of the reasons why British Columbians feel alienated from the federal government percolated through 1971. It resulted in Harold Moffat's resignation from the Northern Development Council – a consortium of mayors in the region who attempted to get political will and appropriate investment lined up to benefit three basic industries: forest products, mining and petroleum and natural gas resources.

In March a brief entitled "Projected Industrial Expansion and Development North of the 52nd Parallel in the Province of British Columbia 1971-1981" was sent to the federal government. In it, the Northern Development Council asked for specific help needed in construction of railroads and highways, construction of port facilities, and development of Townsite planning, roads, water, sanitary and storm sewers, pollution control, recreational facilities, municipal buildings and housing in the regional district of Fraser-Fort George and the city of Prince George.

The specific request was a suggestion that the federal government provide tax incentives or relief to industries to account for the cost differential of establishing in a northern location. Also that the higher cost of living be recognized, and therefore implementation of income tax exemptions or increased retirement benefits be granted to citizens here.

Seven months later, Mayor Moffat finally received indication through the provincial government that nothing was happening. Adding to the frustration was knowledge that two of the regions were not forthcoming with support. He sent this letter, dated October 12, 1971, to the mayors of the North Central Region and also to the chairman of the Regional District:

Dear Sirs:

Enclosed is a copy of a letter I received from the Honourable Ray Williston, which I think should be of interest to those that supported the 1971-1981 Northern Forecast. I have resigned from the Northern Development Council due to the lack of support by two regions to the levy for the brief that sparked the formation, but more important by inability to develop action along more definite lines of priority on the job opportunity level.

I have nothing against the Northern Development Council, it can possibly do much good as an instrument for the interchange of area information between regionals for the good of the whole area, but I feel there is too much divergence of opinion on the guide lines of what is development, to be an effective force.

I felt and still feel that we should define more precisely the order or priorities and without compromise of compassion state a definite position and go back to Ottawa with that statement.

I think we could take the resolutions adopted by the Northern Development Council and set up committees of Mayors from the areas not directly affected to study the proposals and submit final judgment. For instance, on the question of a port on the coast, let the interior Mayors judge from the submissions of the affected areas the priority. On the question of the road to Port Simpson versus paving of Alaska Highway, let the coast Mayors judge the priority.

On the other hand with negotiations going on for running lights on the P.G.E. and C.N.R. maybe we should be developing a study on these implications or maybe we should be taking a definite stand in respect to the equalization of development subsidies for all areas.

Whatever, I shall be interested at any time to participate

with any mayor group that wishes to promote Northern Development on the lines outlined in the brief.

Yours truly, Harold A. Moffat, Mayor

Excerpt from a letter written by the Hon. Ray Williston, Minister of Lands, Forests and Water Resources, dated from Victoria October 5, 1971.

You will recall that a few months ago you and some of your colleagues spearheaded an investigation into the potential opportunities for development within the north-central areas of the province. The general purpose of the study was to show where investment might provide job opportunities and at the same time indicate a fair return of invested capital.

...

The provincial government has not had any positive reaction to the request that was made and I have not learned of any direct reply that has been received by your group from the federal government.

At the time of our interest and presentations we were both requesting that equal treatment should be afforded northern community development in British Columbia compared to that which had been given to specific situations in nearly every other province of Canada.

Within the last couple of weeks a new programme of assistance has been announced for the Gaspé Region of Quebec. This marks a second attempt when a first programme became bogged down after the spending of something more than one hundred million dollars on the paper work without a development involving any physical accomplishment. The new five-year programme commits the expenditure of four hundred eleven million dollars. The population to receive such assistance numbers about 240,000 people.

...

Yours very truly, Ray Williston, Minister

With the fall, attention focussed on the arts community. The Theatre Workshop had just completed its new building at the corner of Highway 16 and the By-Pass (Highway 97) and approached Council for permission to name the building. Their choice was The Prince George Playhouse, which was approved by motion supported by Aldermen Alf Nunweiler and Lorne McCuish at a special Council meeting held on November 9th.

The first week of November 1971 saw the official opening of the $87,650 expansion to the city's library, located then at the corner of Fourth Avenue and Brunswick Street. Mayor Moffat had opposed the expenditure of any funds on the library, and had informed library board chairman Daphne Baldwin that he would not attend the opening. She insisted that he be there, and in compliance with a long-forgotten threat, Mayor Moffat did attend. He told the crowd that he was "eating crow" by opening the addition. Citizen photographer Dave Milne captured the moment as the mayor used scissors to snip the ribbon, watched intently by Daphne Baldwin and chief librarian John Backhouse.

When looking back on the Council's accomplishments for 1971, the library figured in the Mayor's list. Describing it as "a memorable year and truly a year of accomplishment for the City of Prince George" the highlights were deemed to be accomplishment of the boundary expansion involving amalgamation of surrounding areas; creation of the land bank (where the city was the developer, selling lots to individual buyers for ten per cent above development costs); the library expansion; the curb and gutter program; and construction of a multi-purpose building, justice building, museum and expansion of the fairground.

After two years in office, Mayor Moffat faced competition for the job in the December election. Prince George Realtor and businessman, Elroy Garden, declared his candidacy to run for Mayor. In his campaign statement, he indicated that the major priorities should be those related to people—to create a happy and healthy citizenry. To that end, he said he would promote having adequate police and fire protection, pollution control, parks beautification and a Council where free debate would reign. Using the example of the choice of sewage treatment system, he believed that a well-informed Council should be charged with making the decision—not have the choice on such a highly technical matter be put to referendum. In a published statement, he commented:

> In all fairness, where professional engineers do not always agree, how could we expect you who did not have the opportunity to debate and discuss

the subject over a period of eight months like your present Council? I think it would have been grossly unfair to ask you to explain or understand the difference between the two systems.[106]

The Moffat campaign was set out in a lengthy discussion published in the newspaper. It began with the assertion:

I made a promise to you on seeking election to the office of Mayor two years ago that I would make every effort to give prudent consideration to all matters affecting the operation of this city.[107]

Harold then set out the logic he used in coming to the decision of supporting a secondary treatment facility and then gave a full accounting of the associated costs. Putting the information out in that level of detail ensured the subject would become the major issue in the election. He provided it all as "food for thought" and ended his appeal to the voters with:

It is now in your hands to decide whether I have acted in the best interests of the people of Prince George. Yours respectfully, H.A. Moffat.[108]

---

[106] "Moffat, Garden in mayoralty race." The Prince George Citizen 8 December 1971, p. 13.
[107] "Harold Moffat for Mayor of Prince George," The Prince George Citizen, 8 December 1971, p. 30.
[108] Ibid.

Whether that approach resonated with the majority of the voters, or whether the tradition of electing long-time residents as Mayor – the voters returned Harold Moffat for another term. There are some who would argue he won on the force of his personality alone.

1972

For 1972, the Council was comprised of the same Aldermen as the year before except with the addition of Harry Loder and Victor Litnosky, replacing Elroy Garden and Lorne McCuish.

Because residents of Cottonwood Island lived in homes that had no running water, the city investigated the potential of installing a water system. The estimated total cost was $105,000. Residents were sent this letter and short survey in March:

> Under the terms of the Municipality's frontage tax By-law a portion of this amount requires to be paid back by the owners of property abutting these water mains over a twenty year period.

> The frontage tax charges mentioned above would be based on the cost per front foot per year of $.35. This would mean that a sixty foot lot would require an annual payment towards the cost of the main of $21.00 per year. The monthly charge for water would be $3.10 per month, the same charge as that made throughout the Municipality.

Following the installation of the main, the service connections would be installed by the Municipality at a cost per connection of $150.00. This would provide a three-quarter inch connection at the edge of the owner's property. All work connecting this pipe to the building on your lot would be at your expense. It should be pointed out at this time that the Municipality's By-laws permit only one building on the site to be connected to the Municipal water system. In some cases in the Cottonwood Island there are more than one residence on a parcel of property. The owner would have to choose which one is connected to the water system, and the other buildings occupied as residences would have to be removed from the property or vacated.

....

The purpose then of this letter is to ask of you, an owner of property in the Cottonwood Island, to give an indication for the guidance of Council on two questions:

1. Do you wish the water main installed to serve your property?

2. Are you prepared to then pay for and have installed a water service to your home?

(Replies requested by 23 March 1972).[109]

Forms accompanied the letters. Overwhelmingly, they were returned marked NO to both questions.

At the March 27th meeting, an application to purchase was presented for assembling the land which would become the Pine Centre Mall. Gordon Bryant, acting for Kelfor Holdings, presented the plans for the proposed shopping centre which would occupy land then owned by the city, the Crown, and the golf course. The plan called for construction of a 448,000 square foot enclosed mall plus a 12,000 square foot twin movie theatre. The initial approach involved suggestion of an exchange of land of 29.5 acres in District Lot 1427 (which the city later made into Wilson Park) for the twelve acres of city land required by the shopping centre development. Alternatively, Kelfor offered $100,000 cash for the city-owned land.

As the City's Mayor in the mid-1950s, Gordon Bryant had more than a passing familiarity with the city's requirements for developing. After all, he'd put some of those conditions in place. Harold Moffat had regard for the way Bryant conducted business. "He understood the system, knew what he had to arrange, and was well prepared. He never burst

---

[109] Letter dated 9 March 1972 sent to residents of Cottonwood Island.

out no matter how hard you'd twist his tail. He was always calm, cool and collected." [110]

Right away, concern was raised by the Downtown Business Association which expressed objection for the shopping centre development anywhere but in the heart of the City. Mayor Moffat actually agreed with this stand and supported that concern. He was aware of studies in the United States which proved that those cities which allowed large shopping centre development had suffered. Early on, Mayor Moffat travelled to Phoenix to witness an early example of "core death" for himself. He observed that Seattle had suffered the same problem, as downtown areas became deserted when businesses failed or moved out. Once shopping habits and traffic shifted to the malls, the traffic patterns which sustained downtown businesses were forever disrupted. Further, he noted that articles in municipal magazines pointed out the same issues.

Despite objections, progress on the Pine Centre development proceeded unchallenged. The Mayor also resisted the urge to block the development because, on examination, it appeared to be a positive development for the city. There would be no small businesses which would be in direct competition with downtown

---

[110] Gordon Bryant had been Mayor in 1954 and 1955. During that time, he put guidelines in place for city management and planning. With that background, he knew what needed to be arranged and accomplished that before bringing the proposal to Council. Harold Moffat indicated during an interview 12 February 1997 that he respected Bryant's negotiating style.

stores because all the mall tenants were national or multi-national chains. At the June Council meeting, the aldermen voted to sell about 14 acres of City-owned land at the south-east corner of the golf course to the golf club to make its redevelopment possible after losing three fairways to the shopping mall's acreage needs.

At the September 18th meeting, Aldermen Victor Litnosky and Joe Ter Heide proposed in a motion which carried that an amount up to $1,500 be set aside to engage consulting engineers to create the basic design and construction cost estimates for installation of canopies over the sidewalks on Third Avenue and on George Street. The aim was to provide a more comfortable environment for pedestrians by providing respite from the sun in the summer months and a snow and ice-free walking surface during winter.

During October, the expropriation process began regarding 21 parcels of land on Cottownwood Island. Residents were living there in deplorable conditions with no services and in structures that appeared to be shacks or sheds. Most of the residents had accepted the city's offer of an amount representing two and one half times the 1972 assessed value. Despite the rough living conditions and the perennial threat of flooding, there were some who appealed to the City to be allowed to stay.

One resident complained that the buy-back prices were "totally unrealistic and reminiscent of early wild west days." She asserted that people could not even buy a lot from the sale of their homes and had become "refugees in their own country." In response, the city clerk informed the correspondent that:

> With regard to your reference to the City's buy back policy of two and a half times the assessed value, this figure has been acceptable to 57% of the lot owners in the Cottonwood and the City has authorized the expenditure to purchase these properties of over $340,000.00.

and

> ...we have also co-operated very fully with the Welfare Department to assist in the relocation of families who are in receipt of Social Welfare. In this respect the Welfare Worker who has assignments in the Cottonwood Island advises that his case load has dropped from 380 persons in the Cottonwood Island to less than 100. As the total population at the time of the flood was in the region of 600 to 650, the Council were well aware that many of the persons living down there or owning property down there were in need of assistance of all kinds and this assistance had been freely offered and I am glad to say freely accepted by many.[111]

---

[111] Letter from C.P. Pattullo, City Clerk, dated 25 October 1972.

All in all, the expropriation and relocation of people on Cottonwood Island had been a lively and controversial process. Expropriations were handled by Gordon Bryant, Captain Jeffries of The Salvation Army, and Chester Jeffery in his role as City Treasurer. Some expropriated people were extremely hostile and even threatened Mayor Moffat. Those tended to be some independent types who wanted to keep their area – which they called "The Jungle" – and not have anything about their lives interfered with or disrupted. Not everyone reacted that way. "Others came back and thanked me."[112]

A special highlight of 1972 was the visit to Prince George by Governor General Roland Mitchener and Norah Mitchener. The vice-regal couple arrived by train and Harold and Helen Moffat took them on a tour and then had dinner together on their rail coach. "They were a most gracious couple. They came across the north on a rail tour seeing Canada."[113] As this was a low-key, friendly visit, there was no official gift presented from the City.

1973

Council was comprised of the Mayor and six Aldermen: Donald Currie, Carrie-Jane Gray, Victor Litnosky, Harry Loder, Robert Martin and the return of Lorne McCuish. Jack Heinrich,

---

[112] Interview with Harold Moffat 12 February 1997.
[113] Ibid.

Joseph Ter Heide and Alf Nunweiler[114] did not return.

Opening the first Council meeting of the year, Mayor Moffat reflected on the passing of two people whose life and work were important to Prince George. Thinking back on the accomplishments of the previous year, he said:

> Our accomplishments were dulled by the passing of former Mayor Garvin Dezell on February 4th and his Administrative Colleague, City Manager Aaran Thomson on November 11th. It is sad that they could not have been spared to see the realization of those plans they so trustingly laid. How pleased they would be with our new Boundary extension. But such is life. The world stops for no man and I feel it is a further tribute when from our own ranks, we filled the gap step by step. I would like to express Council's appreciation to the Management team for their performance during the year and especially during this period of readjustment.[115]

In that first speech, the Mayor signalled his intention to strike a Technical Study Committee to investigate the feasibility for the City to

---

[114] Alf Nunweiler served as a Prince George Alderman from 1970 to 1972. He served as M.L.A. for the Fort George riding and was Minister of Northern Affairs in the British Columbia government led by the Hon. Dave Barrett.

[115] Minutes of Inaugural Council Meeting, 8 January 1973.

franchise, own, and operate a cable television service.

The canopy program got a push from City Council when the motion proposed by Aldermen Victor Litnosky and Lorne McCuish was passed in April. The provision made was:

> That Council concur with the Committee recommendation that a Local Initiative Scheme be initiated for installation of canopies using an estimated cost of $110.00 per foot and that these canopies be built on the north side of 3rd Avenue between Brunswick Street and the lane west of George Street, on the south side of 3rd Avenue from Victoria Street to Brunswick Street and from Quebec Street to George Street and on the west side of George Street from 3rd Avenue to 4th Avenue except the Northern Hardware building and the Prince George Hotel both of which have existing canopies.[116]

More concern for an arts centre and art gallery was registered, reflected in the November minutes of the Civic Properties and Recreation Commission meeting. The cause was represented by members of the Prince George Arts Centre and the Gallery Advisory Committee. Noted in the official record:

---

[116] Minutes of Regular Council Meeting 30 April 1973.

22 November 1973 - Minutes of the Civic Properties and Recreation Commission meeting. In attendance, members of the Prince George Arts Centre and the Gallery Advisory Committee.

"The need for a proper Art Gallery was stressed by the attending committee. The Art Gallery could be the nucleus of a Cultural - Recreational Centre. Advised that capital funds were available from the Federal Government from the Art Bank. Additional funding could be made available from Provincial Recreational Facilities Fund. A definite need exists for a place for the exhibiting of art, art classes, touring shows and to be able to provide better shows. The Prince George Art Centre is a totally volunteer organization operating in a very small and inadequate facility and occupancy is tenuous at best. Strong feeling that there is a definite need for an Art Gallery and Cultural Centre. The Community Arts Council sees a need for immediate construction of an Art Gallery, including a library and eventually a larger auditorium. The Commission pointed out that they have placed a sum of money in the provisional budget for 1974 and in-depth study as to the needs and priorities of a Cultural Centre. Question as to who should initiate this action and it was the feeling that it should be a joint Commission and Community Arts Council endeavour. It was pointed out that although federal funding for capital construction was available, that there must be local support for the funds and that land must be provided to secure the Federal Funding. It was indicated that Ottawa is sympathetic to Prince George having land available. The maximum funds available federally is one hundred and twenty thousand ($120,000) dollars for a minimum of four thousand square feet of display space being constructed. Continuing operating funds would have to be provided locally thereafter. The Chairman thanked the group for their presentation and concern and advised that this matter would be considered further."

A glimmer of hope for the arts community occurred in December 1973 when City Manager, Chester Jeffery communicated by inter office memo[117] to Bill Woycik, Civic Properties Manager. That memo was to advise Woycik that Council voted at the December 17 meeting "to set aside land for the Art Centre somewhere in the City of Prince George." He further explained that Council did not wish to promise any specific area.

---

[117] Memorandum is dated 18 December 1973.

1974

New faces on Council were Trent Beatty and Howard Lloyd, replacing Victor Litnosky and the late Harry Loder.

Looking back and ahead towards the future, in his first address to Council for 1974, Mayor Moffat proclaimed:

> Our efforts were dulled by the prolonged illness and final passing of our colleague, Harry Loder. He shall be remembered by his service.

> To retiring Alderman Vic, we thank him for his contribution and in an envious way wish him good health to indulge in the many things he missed while being an Alderman.

> The year 1974 could be an Epic Year for this City. Epic in the sense that 1974 could be the last year of boundary expansion in the history of the City of Prince George. Although the problems involved are somewhat disconcerting, the tremendous future of the City dictates that a wider and more defined scope of planning must come under the umbrella of a representative government from the larger area.[118]

After a retrospective on the impact that world energy prices and distance to markets was having on local business, together with the

---

[118] Minutes of Statutory Meeting of Council, 7 January 1974.

uncertainties of supply, the Mayor ended his remarks to Council on a highly upbeat note, anticipating an exciting year ahead:

> However, whatever happens, Prince George is in financially sound shape, due to good management over the years, has modern and up-to-date services, good staff and is well equipped with the best people to remain the top City in Canada in growth and prosperity.[119]

The canopy program was well under way with the structures in place on Third Avenue and George Street. By summer time, some concerns got raised over the colours being chosen and architect Tom West was asked to attend the Council meeting on July 8 to answer that concern. He assured Council that a lot of consideration had been given to the colour, and that a darker stain was chosen because it would wear much longer and be easier to maintain. For those hoping for something brighter and more colourful, he reminded the Council that individual store signs would provide that. After some discussion, Aldermen Donald Currie and Carrie-Jane Gray proposed a motion that the contractor be allowed to proceed with the canopy colour scheme as selected by the architect. It carried and the project carried on.

By September, as the cold months began descending on the city, Mayor Moffat requested that the city administration investigate the

---

[119] Ibid.

feasibility and cost of installing Plexiglas bus shelters for the protection of bus riders.[120] On the surface, that might have seemed like a good idea, but vandals took them down as fast as they were put up. Eventually, the idea was abandoned. Meanwhile, the downtown canopy project was completed by month's end. Council received a letter from the Downtown Business Association congratulating the city and the contractors "on an excellent and rapid construction of the canopies in the downtown centre."[121]

The Downtown Parking commission representatives attended the first Council meeting in December respecting an option to purchase Lots 16 to 19 (then belonging to The Northern Hardware & Furniture Co. and the Moffat family). Mayor Moffat absented himself from the discussion. Council's motion, proposed by Aldermen Carrie-Jane Gray and Howard Lloyd, carried:

> That the City accept the recommendations of the DPC and the option to purchase Lots 16 to 19 inclusive, Block 45, District Lot 343, Plan 1268 to be exercised at the option sum of One Hundred and Fifty Thousand Dollars ($150,000).[122]

---

[120] Minutes of Regular Council Meeting, 16 September 1974.
[121] Minutes of Regular Council Meeting, 7 October 1974.
[122] Minutes of Regular Council Meeting, 2 December 1974.

MAYOR MOFFAT VOTING – ADVANCE POLL 1974

1975

The size of the City Council expanded to ten Aldermen in 1975. Those elected were: Trent Beatty, Carrie-Jane Gray, Howard Lloyd, Robert Martin, Lorne McCuish, Elmer Mercier, Leonard Proppe, Jack Sieb, Art Stauble and Wilma Wellenbrink.

Opening the January 6th Council meeting, Mayor Moffat had an exuberant announcement. "As of this day, a new horizon unfolds for the City of Prince George. This is the eleventh

boundary expansion since incorporation." [123]
While the expansion meant an increase in the
city's tax base, it also brought responsibility for
providing essential services.

In attendance was Alf Nunweiler, Minister
of Northern Affairs in the Provincial Cabinet. He
presented the official copy of the letters patent to
His Worship the Mayor. He brought greetings
and best wishes of Premier Dave Barrett and the
Government of the Province of British Columbia
and offered his government's assistance to the
newly reincorporated Municipality over the
coming years.

The need to create a planning department
for the City of Prince George, in the view of
some, had become acute. At the next meeting,
architect Tom West presented a brief to Council,
using these examples to support his contention:

> 1. On at least four occasions, high
> demands by the consuming public have
> led to major shopping centres being
> developed in locations virtually
> unmindful of any Master Plan;

> 2. The acute housing shortages of the
> early 1960s have left this community
> with a number of poor housing
> developments which are fast becoming
> dehumanizing slums.

---

[123] Between 1954 and 1974, eleven boundary expansions took place.
All of that land had previously been under provincial government
control.

3.   Demand for industrial warehousing space has created industrial areas in the midst of recreational and residential properties.

4.   All of this has produced the need for temporary vehicular traffic patterns and solutions which are becoming unworkable sources of frustration fraught with real physical danger.

Also, and in some measure, because of the above, even the City Center development concept of "Centrum" (whether a workable solution now or not) has been virtually ignored since its acceptance as the basic planning pattern by the original City over eight years ago.[124]

Tom West received an appreciative response from C.P. Pattullo, City Clerk, in which he was informed:

As you are no doubt aware, the creation of a Planning Department has been actively under consideration by Council for some time, but following your submission, certain resolutions were proposed which might speed up the creation of this department.

The Council indicated that they would very much like to obtain the consensus of opinion of the Northern Chapter of

---

[124] Excerpt of brief to Council, 10 January 1975.

the Architectural Institute on the matter of planning, and the Planning Department. Perhaps we can have your comments at an early date so they can be considered during the process of setting up this department.[125]

By the March 10th meeting, Council was focussed on the potential for proceeding with development according to the Community Plan, required by the Letters Patent of the new municipality. Planning Consultant, Des Parker, was called upon to describe the plans for the first phase of development on Cranbrook Hill. He began by indicating that the surveys and planning studies showed a projected population of 22,000 for this area. He estimated that represented approximately the first third of the area's potential. Subdivision plans had provision of areas for a park, a school and a town centre.

Des Parker spoke to the notion of a town centre, describing it as a place for both work and recreation for the community which would eventually reside on Cranbrook Hill. There would also be a shopping centre, a community school and recreation centres along with services like a fire hall and a branch library. The area planned for development comprised 180 acres.

Returning for the regular Council meeting on July 14th, Des Parker was asked to make presentations respecting commercial space and

---

[125] Letter dated 16 January 1975.

a more detailed explanation of the Cranbrook Hill Town Centre Program. He noted that the town centre area was located adjacent to the University Reserve where eventually recreation facilities would be built which would be convenient for residents living nearby to use. His estimate of the population that could be located there as 37,000. At the conclusion of the presentation, he urged Council to allow for integration of commercial, university, recreation and service purposes.

Many Council meetings featured presentations or correspondence with Gordon Bryant, principal of Cal Investments Limited, respecting development of Block 149, known variously as the Miracle Centre project, Project 400, and eventually called Plaza 400 – located on the downtown block bounded by Queensway and George Street between Fourth and Fifth Avenues. Council eventually voted in favour of a motion proposed by Alderman Bob Martin "That approval be given to the Mayor and Clerk to execute this agreement on behalf of the City of Prince George for the development of Block 149."

The agreement was among Her Majesty the Queen, the City, Project 400 and Cal Investments Limited.[126]

1976

The ten Aldermen elected for 1976 all served again for 1977. They were: Trent Beatty,

---

[126] Minutes of Regular Council Meeting, 1 December 1975.

Monica Becott, Victor Litnosky, Robert Martin, Lorne McCuish, Elmer Mercier, Leonard Proppe, Jack Sieb, Arthur Stauble and Donald Wagner.

One of the pressing social issues of the mid-Seventies was the burgeoning welfare roll. In mid-January, Mayor Moffat spoke out about concerns over what he termed "soaring costs" which kept increasing. He pointed out that for 1976, the City of Prince George was expected to contribute almost a million dollars to the province's welfare system. That represented about a ten percent increase over the year before. His concern was over cutting costs; not cutting back on compassion, saying:

> I'm certainly in favour of providing welfare assistance to people who really need it. But, we've relaxed the eligibility requirements for welfare to the point where many people who could be working are drawing welfare instead. There's no excuse for having so many able-bodied people on welfare. There is lots of work that needs doing.[127]

A comprehensive community plan was under development. To support getting input about the most desirable direction for growth, city planner D.N. McDonald presented a draft of questions to be included in a public survey:

---

[127] "Moffat questions welfare system," The Prince George Citizen, 16 January 1976, front page.

1. What, in your opinion, are the major growth or development problems or issues facing PG today?

2. What, in your opinion, are the major constraints affecting the development of PG today and in the near future?

3. What, in your opinion, are the major opportunities affecting community development today and in the near future?

4. What are the top priorities to be addressed now and in the near future regarding community growth and change in PG?

5. How do you feel about the City's current financial policies and position regarding the provision of specific City services and how do you think cost-sharing for major services or other capital works or programs should be worked out amongst all taxpayers?

6. Would you care to list some of the broad goals and development policy proposals relating to community development which you would like to see debated and included in the community plan?

7. How do you perceive the city's future role as a land developer?[128]

---

[128] Memo from D.N. McDonald, City Planner to Mayor and Council, dated 19 January 1976.

Each question had lots of sub-section categories to probe along the lines of the projects and issues of the day.

The subject of tourism and hospitality made the agenda for the first meeting in February. Bill Jones was invited to bring a model and speak to plans for signs to be erected at the entrances to the City. He advised Council that the cost would be about $3,100. A motion proposed by Alderman Bob Martin and supported by Art Stauble carried to the effect that the design be accepted. Council requested that the model be shown to the Chamber of Commerce so that organization could provide input.

The Hon. Hugh Curtis, provincial Minister of Municipal Affairs, attended a special in camera meeting with the Council on July 5, 1976. The subject was a review of the City's capital requirements for recreation, roads, sewer and storm sewers. That year, water and sewer costs approximated $30 million. A potential concern was the Minister's message that the provincial share dollars for water and sewer might not be continued. At that meeting, Mayor Moffat informed the Minister that the Department of Highways should accept responsibility for the road reconstruction being done on feeder roads to bring them up to urban standards. Amalgamation had brought many of those feeder roads within the urban area.

By the end of July, the city was ready to invite bids to design a cultural centre and library. The following invitation was sent to members of the Architectural Institute of B.C.:

The City is looking for ideas on how best to develop a 13 acre site in the heart of Prince George. The Competition is, first, for an esquisse-type presentation that illustrates the competitors concept for the total site development and indicates an acceptable location for the Library and, second, for a fully developed design which best serves the requirements of the Library. It is the intention of the sponsor that the Library be sited and designed in such a way that other facilities can be added progressively over the years in accordance with the master plan concept.

The Jurors are:

Mr. Henry Elder, Emeritus Professor of Architecture, UBC

Mr. T.P. Morris, Architect Planner, Vancouver

Mr. Keith Gordon, Chairman, PG Public Library Board

Mr. D.N. McDonald, City Planner, PG

Mr. Jolyon Briggs, Architect and Professional Advisor

The first prize will be the commission to design the Library. Should the sponsor for any reason decide not to proceed with the work, the successful competitor will receive the sum of fifteen thousand dollars.

The second prize will be five thousand dollars and the third prize three thousand dollars.

The schedule for the Competition is as follows:

Invitations issued	July 26, 1976
Conditions released	August 9
Closing date for questions	September 10
Closing date for registration	September 10
Submission of entries	November 5, 1976 at 4:30[129]

There was keen interest amongst the architectural design community. Within two months, an overwhelming 104 indicated an interest in preparing designs. The previous December, Council had invited two prominent British Columbia architects to serve as judges for the library design competition along with Prince George-based architect, Jo Briggs. They were Henry Elder, professor emeritus, and former head of the School of Architecture at the University of British Columbia (then retired to Salt Spring Island), and T.P. Morris, an architect and planner associated with the Canadian Housing and Mortgage Corporation, based in Vancouver.

---

[129] Letter to Architectural Institute of B.C. dated 26 July 1976.

Council celebrated the news from the provincial government in August that construction grants of $320,498 for the Elkscentre Arena and $289,647 for the Kin II Arena had been approved.[130]

At the end of the year, the city was provided with preliminary population counts for the 1976 Census of Canada. Ottawa-based statisticians had determined that Prince George had a population of 59,323 people. As of June 1, 1976, there were 19,083 private dwellings, and of those, 1,460 were unoccupied.[131]

1977

The Library's budget for the year ahead came under scrutiny in January. Board Chairman, Keith Gordon, accompanied Librarian John Backhouse forming a delegation to the Council meeting. The first salvo was fired by Alderman Lorne McCuish who inquired "whether items could not be shaved down during this period of restraint?" Other suggestions for finding revenue were discussed, including the possibility of charging Library users. That was quelled after it was pointed out that the Provincial Libraries Act precluded charging for the use of books and reference materials. Another suggestion to reduce the book budget met strong opposition. Alderman Art Stauble

---

[130] Letter from the Hon. Grace McCarthy, Minister of Recreation and Travel Industry to W.E. Woycik, General Manager, Civic Properties and Recreation Committee, dated 10 August 1976.
[131] Letter from R.A. Wallace, Assistant Chief Statistician, to David N. McDonald, City Planner, dated 2 December 1976.

brought up the fact that the overall City budget had been held to a 10% increase and raised expectation that the Library "could look at possible reductions." The fractious discussion was mercifully ended with a motion proposed by Bob Martin and seconded by Elmer Mercier that the budget for the Library Board be approved. It carried[132].

In March, Burnaby-based television station BCTV began broadcasting a series of unflattering and inflammatory claims on the subject of land development in Prince George. The accusations had been started by an Edmonton-based development group which had bought up land in the Blackburn area. Subsequently, City Council had redesigned the area. Their specific issue was that the sewer line had been run up Gunn Road, and the Alberta developers began to allege that the decision had been made to help the Moffats. A Realtor named Qu'appelle had been providing information to those developers which caused them to believe that the City might not be able to supply water to that land and that their investment would be frozen out.

Once the first accusations were featured on BCTV's News Hour, events began to cascade. On April 4, 1977 one of the station's cameramen, Dale Hicks, came to City Hall a few hours in advance of the Council meeting. He hand-delivered a letter to the Assistant City Clerk asking for permission to film the Council

---

[132] Excerpts from Minutes of the Regular Council Meeting, 24 January 1977.

meeting that evening, without sound. The request was for permission to capture images of people who were making decisions concerning the City's future direction. When the Council meeting opened and the correspondence was communicated, Alderman Victor Litnosky believed the request acceptable and, supported by Donald Wagner, moved that permission be granted. The motion went down to defeat with Mayor Moffat and Aldermen Becott, Proppe, Stauble, Beatty and Martin voting against it.

By the end of the month, it became apparent that the attack on the integrity and reputation of the Mayor and members of Council was serious. At the last regular Council meeting of April, Aldermen Jack Sieb and Monica Becott proposed that Vancouver lawyer Allan McEachern of Russell DuMoulin be engaged to secure copies of the recent BCTV show tapes which featured the subject of recent land deals. That motion carried unanimously. Discussion followed indicating that Council's sentiment was that the damage done to the City's reputation was more important than the costs of defending it.[133]

Two days later, at the request of Aldermen Lorne McCuish and Trent Beatty, a Special Council Meeting convened. The purpose was to put in motion formal engagement of Allan McEachern to provide legal advice and commence legal action against BCTV. The notes taken record this sentiment:

---

[133] Minutes of Regular Council Meeting, 26 April 1977.

The series, couched in misstatement and slanted viewpoints and based on undocumented statements of persons not having the courage to identify themselves, is causing irreparable damage to the elected Council of the City, to its Administrators and Employees, and to the citizens of Prince George. The telecasting rights held by BCTV are granted by the CRTC, and every and all breaches of broadcasting regulations should be reported by Mr. McEachern to the CRTC so that they may properly consider cancellation of the BCTV licence.[134]

As the result of advice presented by legal counsel, Council passed the following motion proposed by Aldermen Lorne McCuish and Bob Martin:

That Council endorse the resolution outlined in Mr. McEachern's report and authorize Mr. McEachern to bring an action on behalf of the City of PG against BCTV in the Supreme Court of British Columbia, for damages for libel unless BCTV broadcasts an appropriate contradiction or explanation in terms satisfactory to City Council.[135]

The motion carried with only Aldermen Litnosky and Mercier voting against.

---

[134] Notes from Special Council Meeting, 28 April 1977.
[135] Minutes of Regular Council Meeting, 27 June 1977.

Later in that meeting, Council entertained a petition of 196 signatures requesting that Wilson Park continue to be used for motor cycle sports. Gordon Bryant was there to speak against this, and urged Council to find another area for the sport so neighbouring residents would not be affected by the noise.[136] The petition carried the day with two (Aldermen Elmer Mercier and Donald Wagner) voting against it.

At the first Council meeting in December 1977, Mayor Moffat broke with tradition and recited an impressive litany of accomplishments. He did that because it was the end of the term for the Aldermen whose terms were ending, and he believed they should be in attendance while the accomplishments were remembered.

The Mayor indicated that the most significant effort of 1977 was to expand fire protection to cover the whole City, including the recently amalgamated areas. Beyond that, he listed:

> the City Hall expansion
> the purchase of the Danson estates property
> purchase of the Forestry Buildings
> initiation of the Transit Study
> Blackburn Sewer
> R.A.P. and N.I.P program for Peden Hill
> expanded dog control and additional facilities

---

[136] This was a curious stand for Gordon Bryant, a motorcyclist himself, to take!

purchase of the private property around
sewage disposal site
establishment of a City Planning
department
enlargement of Building Inspection
department
Water District amalgamation
Staff integration
rezoning of South Fort George and V.L.A.
establishment of Highway corridors
the banking proposals
steel mill study
computer program
garbage pickup expansion
Nechako sewer
the building of the Kin II Centre
the Livestock Arena
paving of the areas adjacent to the
Livestock Arena
the Elkscentre and Gordon Road Park
development
the Kelly Road School
Firehall extension
Vanway firehall
the Second Avenue Parkade

Project 400

The City and Province have agreed on a
road upgrading plan, which has already
begun, including the upgrading of the
Bypass Highway, the construction and
paving of Foothills and asphalting of
many roads within the new City.

Water will be furnished to the Lafreniere and the Parkridge areas, to the Danson Estates and adjacent area, plus sewage disposal for the latter. A storm drainage study has been developed for North Nechako, Blackburn and south west sector. Blackburn has also received a new water well. Construction is underway on a Storm Drainage Trunk system which will drain Peden Hill and the whole Cranbrook Hill area. Most of the land has been acquired for the Ospika extension, plus much of the Foothhills and the road allowances for the Blackburn long range plans.

You will miss the Bridge and Community Plan decisions; however, the

  zoning By-law
  Licensing By-law
  Offsite Capital Headworks Levy
  Cultural Study and Architectural
  Competition, and
  Assessment Formula

were all decisions that were made during your office.

Besides being proud of your accomplishments, I know you will join with me in congratulating our Administration and staff for their efforts that made all this possible.

On behalf of the citizens, I thank you for your contribution and wish you well in your divers concerns.

To the new members, a warm welcome to a most active future. The budget, the Community Plan and a complementary Zoning By-Law will fill in much of your spare time for the next year.

Respectfully submitted, Harold A. Moffat, Mayor[137]

Council reconvened the next week for a special Budget Committee meeting. On the agenda were grant requests of $7,928 for the Prince George Art Gallery and $6,882 for Studio 2880. On a supporting motion from Aldermen George Gibbins and Monica Becott, both grants were approved. Mayor Moffat recorded that he was opposed, even nine days before Christmas![138] Other grants which received unanimous support from Council were $26,500 (distributed over a five year period) for the Prince George Theatre Workshiop; $28,550 for the Chamber of Commerce to support tourism development; and $2,700 for the Community Arts Council. Also approved, but with an opposing vote from the Mayor was $344,873 for the Library for book acquisition. As he recorded his vote against this expenditure, Mayor Moffat said he believed there should be a way to make people pay for damaging books.

---

[137] Minutes of Regular Council Meeting, 5 December 1977.
[138] Notes from Budget Committee meeting, 16 December 1977.

1978

Composition of the ten-member Council changed for 1978 with the return of four from the year before: Monica Becott, Jack Sieb, Art Stauble and Donald Wagner. The other six were new: Ed Bodner, Brian Brownridge, George Gibbins, Richard Godfrey, Stuart Ross, and Dale Steward.

Among the first issues dealt with at the inaugural meeting was the need for a soup kitchen in the George Street area. Anna Roe, group organizer of volunteers for the Diocese of Prince George approached Council by letter about permission and space to operate from 7:30 to 12:30 on Friday nights. Aldermen Monica Becott and Art Stauble supported a motion that Anna Roe be invited to make a presentation at the next meeting.

Phase I of the Library was ready to proceed by the February 13th meeting with architect Graham Tudor's winning model of the Cultural Centre on display and architect Jo Briggs in attendance to explain the proposal and answer questions. Council supported the suggestion proposed by Aldermen Art Stauble and Bob Martin that the Library Committee reconvene to study the proposed design and recommend any modifications needed.

At the first Council meeting in March, the Library project was begun when Aldermen Ed Bodner and Art Stauble put forward the motion:

That the City of Prince George enter into a contract with Graham Tudor (Architect) for the design and construction supervision of the proposed new library facility.

That motion was carried with the expected and anticipated vote in opposition cast by Mayor Moffat.[139]

Transportation issues percolated to the top of Council's agenda in March with delegations attending from the Ministry of Highways. With Prince George M.L.A. Howard Lloyd in attendance, discussion focussed on selection of an alternate bridge crossing for the Nechako River. Lloyd was in favour of Foothills boulevard. Before adjournment, a unanimously-supported motion (put forward by Aldermen Jack Sieb and Brian Brownridge) was voted:

That the proposed Foothills alignment be established as the City's number one priority for an alternate Nechako River crossing; and that the Ministry of Highways be requested to commence design and proceed with construction of the Foothills bridge and approaches thereto.[140]

The next month, Russell DuMoulin, solicitors for the City of Prince George, submitted advice by correspondence that Judge Toy had found in favour of the City of Prince

---

[139] Minutes of Regular Council Meeting 6 March 1978.
[140] Minutes of Regular Council meeting, 13 March 1978.

George in the case which had been brought against BCTV. There was notice that BCTV had filed an appeal, and further action would be determined by that outcome. The correspondence was received, awaiting final resolution of the case.[141]

With the fall meetings, Council heard presentations from Jim Ellis, real estate representative for McDonald's Restaurants Ltd. respecting plans to establish three locations in Prince George. The first was planned for the corner of Victoria and 20th Avenue with the second one at the corner of Massey and Westwood.

Architect Graham Tudor attended the December 20th meeting and responded to any concerns expressed by the Design Panel for the new Library building. The brief version was this description:

> The plans provide for a library of 32,000 square feet to be set on top of two levels of parking with a capacity of 139 cars. Entry to the Library is made via internal staircase and an elevator or via a pair of ramps in front of the building leading from passenger drop-off area set in a raised landscaped park setting. The Library program itself includes a children's area, audio visual services, multi-purpose room, adult reference

---

[141] Minutes of Regular Council Meeting, 3 April 1978.

library, periodical area and local history room.[142]

End of the Moffat Administration

As the 1979 municipal election approached, Harold Moffat had made his decision that he would not run for another term. "I was getting pressure to pull my weight at the store. My boys wanted me to come back and believed I should be there at least from 2:00 p.m. to 5:00 p.m. every day."[143]

Regarding his nine years in the Mayor's chair, from the perspective of twenty years later, he was satisfied that he accomplished what he had in mind when he first expressed interest in managing the city's business. "I made sure the City was set on a plan, not just going along reacting to what was happening. At that time, people could look at the maps and see what we had in mind for services like roads, water and sewer."[144]

A particularly satisfying stand was Council's management over Pine Valley. During his time as Mayor, Harold dealt with some developers who wanted to alter the Official Community Plan. Never a fan of developers at the best of times, he thought the plan to wipe out Pine Valley and make it all a commercial

---

[142] Document from Prince George Advisory Design Panel, 20 December 1978.
[143] Interview with Harold Moffat 24 February 1997.
[144] Ibid.

area was particularly odious. Others felt just as strongly, and several thousand signatures were collected. Commercial development was forestalled, and the result was a very attractive community golf course.

Although there is certainly a ceremonial aspect to the Mayor's job, that isn't what appealed to Harold. He didn't particularly enjoy the "frills" or "perks" of office and attended only those dinners where he was required, as Mayor, to be at the head table. Otherwise, his strong preference was to have dinner at home. "I wore the chain of office for pictures and for the inauguration ceremony each year, but otherwise, I didn't wear it at meetings."[145] Friend and broadcaster Bob Harkins also noticed that Harold didn't fit the mold. "He wore an old cardigan and tie and was not into parading any formality of the office."[146]

Bob said there were many times when they didn't agree on issues, but he had the utmost respect for Harold as a square shooter and someone who didn't hold a grudge. He explained that by describing him this way:

> Harold could be an adversary politically, but at the end of the day, he would turn a new page in the book. I respect him. His integrity is uncompromised. How he sees himself is what matters. He sets high standards for himself ethically

---

[145] Ibid.
[146] Interview with Bob Harkins, 30 January 1997.

and morally. He's a fair man. He's helped a lot of people and does it in the shadow of his father.[147]

As a journalist covering city hall for years, Bob got interviews with Harold when no one else could. "Harold was never around on election night. I would find him out at his horse barn near the airport. He wasn't trying to hide—it's just what he did. He'd talk to anybody who'd come out to see him there."[148]

For Harold, the enjoyable aspect of being Mayor was the debates. "I enjoyed that. I delighted in the arguments. Lots of times you had to throw out the fishing line and the bait to see if anybody would take it up."[149] And, of all the aldermen he served with, who gets remembered as the best arguers? Harold says that Jack Heinrich, Art Stauble and Trent Beatty could always be counted upon to put up a good argument. He also could depend on Bob Martin to speak up with the socialist New Democratic perspective to joust against Harold's own conservative Social Credit sensibilities. What might seem like knock-down-drag-'em-out fights were actually intense and often witty exchanges. "We had respect for one another."[150]

As for the greatest accomplishment, Harold believes that was the amalgamation of surrounding areas (South Fort George, College

---

[147] Ibid.
[148] Ibid.
[149] Interview with Harold Moffat 24 February 1997.
[150] Ibid.

Heights and the Hart Highway area) which all came under the city's jurisdiction in 1975.[151] For him, the next most important was development and implementation of an official community plan.[152] Production of that document dominated the work of his last year in office and, with amendments, continues to be used by the city government.

Epilogue to the Mayor Years . . .

For nine years in the 1970s, from the beginning of 1970 to the end of 1978, Prince George was led by one of its icons. Born in 1915, the same year the city was incorporated, people who know Harold Moffat know they can equate the age of the city with his. After all, he and the city grew up together.

He's known this place in its infancy, with horses clopping down Third Avenue when it was little more than a dirt and gravel lane framed by board sidewalks. He's seen businesses come and go, and devoted his working life to the hardware and furniture business started by his father in 1919. He's known all the true characters who ever lived here and knows that he's one of them.

And there is something in this society that rankles people when an icon comes under attack. That is how many reacted when BCTV, the powerful media corporation which has more

---

[151] "Ex-mayor celebrates along with city," 6 March 2000, front page.
[152] The plan was required by the Municipal Act, and gave an overall perspective concerning how the city should be developed.

influence than any other communications medium in this province, set out to attack the solid and dignified reputation of Harold Moffat.

As someone who lived his life according to the old world standards by which he was raised, it had been an unsettling and hurtful experience to be accused of any wrongdoing.

The accusations came out of claims made in an undated, unsigned document addressed to the attention of the Attorney General of British Columbia, marked "Confidential." It was crudely typed, double-spaced on 8 ½" x 14" paper with comical spelling errors and erratic punctuation. In ten and a half pages, the authors asked for a public judicial inquiry accusing the Mayor, Council and Regional District representatives of wrongdoing "for their personal long and short term benefits or gains." At the end the words printed were: "A Dozen Concerned Civic Employees."

Since the television news broadcasts occurred in April 1977, it is presumed that the accusing document was provided to media contacts immediately prior to that time. To redeem his personal reputation, Harold filed a law suit against BCTV.

Closing that case took seven years and involved expensive big-city lawyers arguing back and forth by couriered letters. With the station requesting and getting many deferrals, the case was kept dragging on. Eventually, the television station had to admit that they had made a mistake. Less than a week before the trial was to proceed, David Gooderham, one of the lawyers acting for BCTV contacted Harold's lawyer, Glen Parrett, and indicated willingness to settle out of court. It was Glen Parrett who demanded and got an official, formal apology. It was read on the BCTV News Hour, broadcast to the entire province.

Sitting in the television studio, anchorman Tony Parsons fixed his sincere brown eyes on the TelePrompTer and read the longest statement ever delivered from the anchor desk:

> One of British Columbia's longest running libel actions has come to an end today. The action was commenced seven years ago by Harold Moffat, then Mayor of the City of Prince George. It arose out of an eight part broadcast series prepared by BCTV in April of that year. Prince George at that time was nearing the end of a lengthy real estate boom which had led to extensive land speculation and development in the Prince George area. BCTV's series of broadcasts drew attention to windfall profit by developers, escalating costs of residential building lots and possible conflicts of interest involving a number of persons including then Mayor Harold Moffat.
>
> Then Mayor Harold Moffat believed he had been seriously wronged by the broadcast, brought an action for libel

against BCTV. After winding its way through the court process it was set to proceed to trial October 29th, 1984 at Prince George.

While BCTV believed it was fulfilling its mandate in broadcasting what it believed was an important story on a matter of public interest, BCTV at no time intended to imply that the then Mayor Harold Moffat had done anything wrongful in carrying out his duties as mayor. In fact, a subsequent police investigation made no finding of any wrongdoing on the part of Harold Moffat.

The first transaction questioned by BCTV as giving rise to a conflict of interest involving Mayor Moffat was in 1973. BCTV reported that Mayor Moffat had persuaded City Council to suspend negotiations on the purchase of 160 acres of land to the west of the city and reported that one week later the land was purchased by a friend of the Mayor who immediately resold the property for a profit in excess of $170,000.00. A thorough review of the in camera minutes of City Council meetings at that time which have recently become available reveal that council had instructed the City Manager to continue negotiations. That followed a motion in which three council members including

Moffat had rejected a $500.00 option to purchase the property. The Mayor states that he opposed the option because he wanted to await a report by the planning consultant expected in a week regarding the long term planning for Cranbrook Hill. The minutes say that the decision on the purchase would probably be reached after that report.

A further development which BCTV questioned whether it gave rise to a conflict of interest was the extension of the Blackburn sewer line to an area known as Airport Hill, where a sewer line also reached a point adjacent to a large acreage of property owned by a company known as Northern Hardware, in which the then Mayor Harold Moffat held a one-eighth interest. BCTV raised this in its broadcast series, as an example of the kind of possible conflicts of interest that might exist. Mayor Moffat thought he was treated unfairly in that the broadcast at one point identified the land as being owned by him personally and was being rezoned. As Mr. Moffat has rightly pointed out the land was in fact owned by a company controlled by his family in which he was a one-eighth shareholder and was not being rezoned. The broadcast went on to state that Mayor Moffat's portion with the sewer extension and rezoning would be worth

$8,000,000.00 when divided and resold. In fact there has been no such rezoning and the estimated value at that time in the condition it was then in was approximately $160,000.00.

Former Mayor Moffat states that the policy he supported for sewers going into the area was to alleviate long existing problems in the area and not to encourage major development. The land in Blackburn that was the subject of the original broadcast series has not been developed.

He has also expressed concern that while showing city equipment working on privately owned land, including land owned by Northern Hardware, it did not state that the Northern Hardware paid the City of the full costs involved.

Mayor Moffat also felt strongly about the fact that the broadcast dealt with the extension of the sewer line to lands known as "Autumn Estates," which were owned by a company controlled by Stewart Wood. Mr. Moffat thought that in order to have given a balanced view the broadcast should have pointed out that he as Mayor and as a member of the Regional District Board had previously voted against removing these same lands from the Agricultural Land Reserve and wrote a dissenting report.

The original series of broadcasts also indicated that full and final approval for the Autumn Estates subdivision was granted by Prince George City Council on November 29th, 1976 and that when built and sold it would yield a profit of one and a half million dollars to Mr. Wood. The broadcast did not include a description of the complicated conditions imposed in the land use contract granted to Autumn Estates or any description of the conditional nature of their land use contract. The conditions imposed in the land use contract were not fulfilled and no work was ever done with respect to that subdivision.

At the conclusion of BCTV's broadcast seven years ago, BCTV noted that there was a criminal investigation proceeding conducted by the RCMP Commercial Crime Section. The investigation did look into a number of matters raised in the broadcast along with matters relating to the alleged land deals. Harold Moffat opened his records to the investigators. At the conclusion of that investigation there was no finding of any wrongdoing on the part of Harold Moffat.

Former Mayor Moffat has now retired from his forty years of public service.

The television station also bought advertising space in the Prince George Citizen to run the text of the statement on two days. The first was published on Friday, October 26, 1984 on the second page. BCTV also paid Harold's legal costs.[153]

Harold explained to the Citizen that he did not seek any monetary settlement and only had interest in having his name cleared. "I just wanted them to admit they didn't investigate both sides. They just took one side and thought they had a scoop, and they went off half-cocked."[154]

However, it remains true that an apology or a retraction doesn't make any injustice right; nor does it remove the devastating effect on the person accused and his family. Also, not all those who heard the accusations ever became aware of the statement.

It is interesting to know that BCTV learned from the experience. Ever since, there is much greater care taken in determining the veracity of information provided, and the ramifications of making a mistake are now very well understood.

Decades later, those circumstances are easily recalled by Tony Parsons. "I remember that incident and reading the apology on air. To this day, whenever we goof up in the news room

---

[153] "BCTV to pay legal costs," The Vancouver Sun, 27 October 1984, p. A13.
[154] "BCTV airs statement: Moffat's name cleared," Prince George Citizen, 26 October 1984, front page.

– and we don't do that very often – we say to each other, 'We've got a Harold Moffat.'"[155]

---

[155] Conversation with Tony Parsons, 9 November 1997.

Chapter VIII

Managing The Northern Hardware & Furniture Co. Ltd.

The Beginning

A.B. Moffat's first job in Fort George was sawing wood for 25 cents a cord. His next job was as a timekeeper for the Department of Public Works, making him an employee of the provincial Conservative governments headed by Richard McBride (until December 1915) and by William John Bowser (until November 1916).

With the November 1916 election, political winds shifted in British Columbia and a Liberal government was elected under the leadership of Harlan Carey Brewster who died in office after serving as premier for just 16 months. Following that, John Oliver was elected and led the government until 1927. When the government changed, A.B. Moffat lost his job. His next employment was with a survey party that went out to locate a more direct route between Fraser Lake and Vanderhoof. At Fraser Lake, he obtained a pre-emption on a quarter section of land, and used that as collateral to borrow $500.00. The cash was needed to establish his business venture with partner Frank Whitmore. Together, they purchased the Northern Mercantile and Lumber Co. in January 1919.

Two months later, the business partners published this advertisement:

<u>To the Buying Public</u>

We wish to announce that we have purchased the Hardware Business of the Northern Lumber and Mercantile Co. Ltd. of this city.

We carry a full line of Stoves, Ranges, Automobile Accessories, Builders', Trappers', and Prospectors' Supplies, etc. and beg to take this opportunity of soliciting your patronage.

Yours in anticipation,
The Northern Hardware Co.
A.B. Moffat
F.W. Whitmore[156]

ADVERTISEMENT 30 APRIL 1919

---

[156] Advertisement published 19 March 1919, Prince George Citizen, p.3.

Store Locations
The Northern was located on:

1. George Street (takeover of Northern Lumber Company, renamed Northern Hardware in 1919).
2. George Street at Third Avenue.
3. The north-west corner of 3rd and Quebec.
   Bay location (later the Zeller's location on 3rd Avenue) The Bay moved in when the Northern moved out.
4. Present location at 1386 Third Avenue at Brunswick.

THROUGH THE DECADES AT THE STORE

The 1920s

George Street

In the early years, the Northern Hardware served as the major supplier to those working in the three main occupations of the area—the loggers; the prospectors and the farmers who established homesteads.

Other businesses in downtown Prince George which were in existence when the Northern was established in 1919 were:

Sterling Meat Market
Spanner's Men's Wear
Bryce Parker Men's Wear
Ivor Guest
C.C. Reid's Groceries
Gordon Woods, druggist

Fred Taylor's Pool Hall
and, up the street, the Ford Motor
Company was owned and operated by Ed
Hall.

There was not a lot of competition for the
Northern Hardware which started out in
business offering hardware, furniture and
appliances. There was only one drygoods store
in town, Hughes & Drake which became Hughes
& Ratledge. Elsewhere in Prince George, John
McInnis and Pete Anderson sold building
supplies.

During the spring of 1920, The Northern's
business was brisk enough to warrant
construction of a warehouse 20 feet by 70 feet.
The structure was built on Third Avenue East by
contractor A.P. Anderson. The building was
near completion by the end of March.

By 1921, The Northern became the regional
agent for John Deere farm implements. The
Northern ran large illustrated ads with
descriptive content:

There is a John Deere Plow For You

No matter what kind of soil you have
there is a John Deere plow made for it.
Deere & Company make 800 different
styles of plows to meet the requirements
of farmers in all parts of the world.
Location makes no difference. All you
have to do is to pick out a plow suitable
for your farm.

There is a John Deere Plow For Every man

For 70 years these plows have been the standard of the world. There is a high-grade quality about them that you can't explain but you "feel" it every time you plow with a John Deere.

John Deere Invented the Steel Plow.

Gold Medal at every World's Fair or International Exposition since 1840.[157]

Along with that, the range of garden supplies and tools was regularly advertised. Included in stock were three complete lines of garden seeds – McKenzie, Ferry and Rennie. The tool assortment was spades, shovels, hoes, rakes, spading forks, brush scythes, brush hooks, mattocks, grub hoes, garden cultivators and trowels. Customers were invited to come in to see the stock or inquire by telephone. The store's phone number was 91.

Tragedy struck the family in that year. A.B. Moffat's wife, Emma, died in June from complications relating to childbirth. Their newborn son died in Quesnel three months later in September after a short illness. A.B. subsequently married Florence Avis Horwood who bore eight children. In order of birth they were: Raymond Keith Moffat May 25, 1924; Gordon Lorne Moffat, September 14, 1925;

---

[157] Advertisement published 1 April 1921, The Prince George Leader, p. 3.

Vernon Donn Moffat, May 24, 1927; Betty Mae Moffat, July 25, 1928; Clifford Earl Moffat, September 21, 1929; John Eldon Moffat, July 7, 1931; Gilbert Horwood Moffat, August 17, 1932; and Joyce Kathleen Moffat, March 5, 1937.

For Christmas shoppers in 1923, The Northern ran large ads with gift suggestions of practical hardware-type items like flashlights and pocket knives. More appealing gift suggestions were 1847 Rogers silverware, sold as complete place settings or individually; and 97-piece dinner sets in Royal vitreous china for $35.00. Coffee percolators, electric irons, and reading lamps powered by gasoline or electricity also were on offer. For children, The Northern carried a supply of hockey skates and shoes. At that time, the skates were just blades which had to be attached to the shoes or boots. Winter sleighs ranged in price from $1.00 to $4.25. A truly prized gift would have been the Marswell's electric washer – a thoroughly modern contraption in 1923.

By the Christmas season of 1926, The Northern expanded the number of models carried for radio receiving sets. Big and boxy, they brought news of the world and entertainment into people's homes. The Northern's ads urged customers to make 1926 "a radio Christmas" and invited them to come in to hear the Radiola Super-Heterodyne model before buying. The store carried a full line of radio parts (think large glass replacement tubes!), batteries and battery eliminators.

As electrical appliances became available, they appeared in this order: radios, electric toasters, washing machines, and airtight heaters.

The Northern Hardware had an optimistic start to the year in January 1928. The furniture end of the business was begun as a necessity. The Northern Hardware Co. expanded its horizons and became The Northern Hardware & Furniture Co. Ltd.

The company announced its purchase of the post office block with plans to renovate that building and open a furniture business by the following spring. Originally, the intent was to operate two separate stores in Prince George. The renovations were completed sooner than expected, and the furniture store was ready for business at the beginning of November. An ambitious first shipment included a selection of chesterfield suites, nesting tables, upholstered chairs, dining room suites and bedroom furniture. Top brands of the day were names like McLagan's, Moore-Bell Ltd., Farquarharson-Gifford and Malcolm Hills. Advertising took a non-threatening approach with statements like this: "We cordially invite you to step in and look it over. You will be under no obligation to buy."[158]

The Northern's biggest line was Restmore from Vancouver. Their mattress line was called

---

[158] Advertisement published 16 August 1928, Prince George Citizen, p. 4.

Rip Van Winkle. Most other mattress suppliers (like Simmons) and furniture suppliers were from Eastern Canada. Duty killed looking to American suppliers. Carloads of stoves and general steelware came in from Eastern Canada. The Northern sold a lot of washtubs, enamelware, ranges and heaters. The store also shipped west to Prince Rupert. The goods came by rail from across Canada to Prince Rupert, and then were supposed to be sent back to Prince George. This seemed an unnecessary round trip in practical terms, so there was an arrangement made to offload when the train came through Prince George.[159] Deliveries had to be shipped on paper through Prince Rupert, though, to obtain the most favourable freight rates.

The Northern also built a reputation for carrying quality paint. The brand of the day was "B-H" (Brandram-Henderson) – which was imported from England. The ad copy read "Guaranteed to contain genuine white lead and pure white zinc, combined in the ideal proportions of 70 to 30, forming the strongest covering pigment known to science."[160] The other major brand was Sherwin-Williams paints and varnishes.

---

[159] Historical note: The rails were completed 27 Januaary 1914. The first train arrived in Prince George on January 30th and the first train out of Prince George left on 3 February 1914.

[160] Advertisement published 27 June 1929, The Prince George Citizen, p. 4.

What began as a partnership had grown into a sizeable operation and needed to be formally incorporated. That occurred November 9, 1928.[161] Once it was noticed that the name had been mis-spelled as "Northren" an application for change was made December 28, 1928 as The Northern Hardware & Furniture Company Limited. Management salaries were set at $400.00 per month, but were cut in half once the Depression took hold.

The 1930s

345 George Street

Despite the onset of a continent-wide economic turndown, which later on was referred to as the Depression, The Northern's business survived and the store extended credit to other businesses and customers. When possible, the store operated using a barter system with many of its customers. People traded goods like firewood and farm produce for needed supplies.

Those who required boats to earn their livelihood or wanted them for recreation looked to the line of Johnson outboard motors brought in to the George Street store. In the spring of 1930, The Northern carried a complete stock of Johnson parts and had staff capable of servicing all Johnson engines.

As A.B. Moffat's oldest son, Harold started working at The Northern in the early 1930s. His

---

[161] The B.C. Gazette noted that the Northern Hardware & Furniture Company Limited had an authorized capital of $50,000 with Prince George named as location of its head office.

first job paid $5.00 a week plus board, and from that he had to buy his own lunch. The 1933 provincial election saw Liberal Duff Pattullo elected as premier. He brought in legislation which changed the minimum wage which went from $5.00 to $9.00 a week. Harold remembers that his dad didn't like that!

Harold's first store responsibilities came at that George Street location. The store handled kerosene, gasoline, linseed oil, turpentine, Mobil oil – all in the back. It was Harold's job to get the gas and oil, and then buy whiskey bottles which were washed and filled with turpentine. All the brothers started off working for the store that way.

The next job was working on the delivery truck. That was considered a choice thing to do because of the freedom of being able to travel about doing deliveries, and then having transportation by taking the truck home.

The store used to close on Wednesdays at 1:00 p.m. That would be the time for maintenance chores like oiling the wooden floors. Later, the flooring was battleship linoleum which was imported from England. In an interesting comparison of shipping costs, there was more expense involved in getting those rolls of flooring up to Prince George from Vancouver than what it cost to come by boat from England, through the Panama Canal, and up to the port of Vancouver.

While the decade-long period of economic struggle continued elsewhere, during that time the bright spot economically for this region was gold mining in the Cariboo. Gold was found in the quartz, and people were attracted to jobs at the mine. During that period many people moved from Prince George to Wells. In 1933, The Northern opened a store in Quesnel in premises leased from Paul Krestenuk. The initial lease was for two years at the rate of $45.00 per month. From that location, The Northern serviced Wells using travelling salesmen. A.B. Moffat's partner, Frank Whitmore[162], ran that store and also a Shell Oil agency. It became one of Harold's responsibilities to go to Quesnel in the winter and relieve Bill Willis.

Disaster struck on Boxing Day 1933 when fire consumed the building next door to The Northern's location on George Street. There was some smoke damage, but most of the hardware stock was not affected. However, that event precipitated the move to the next location in the fall of the following year.

George Street at Third Avenue (as of the fall of 1934)
In September 1934, The Northern Hardware took out a three-year lease on the building on the north-west corner of Third Avenue and George Street, with an option to extend that a further two years. Renovations began

---

[162] Management salaries in 1932 were $200.00 per month.

immediately in preparation for moving from the store's original George Street location.

Around that time, Third Avenue was becoming the main street as it connected with the train station. Earlier, George Street had been the centre of the action. When A.B. Moffat relocated the store to Third Avenue, it took courage to move there. Deliveries into Prince George came by boat and rail, but the boat transportation business failed because it couldn't compete with the trains.

In the early years, people were careful with money. They didn't use the telephone very much, and nor did Harold's father, even though the store had a telephone, and he was a shareholder in the Northwest Telephone Company. Instead, he would come in and write letters to accomplish business transactions.

Goods arrived at the store's warehouses in Quesnel and Prince George. Harold's recollection is that the first refrigerator that came into the city was sold to Dr. Ewert. The LCL[163] rate was charged for transport on it, which was the highest.

During uncertain economic times, service at The Northern was maintained to regular standards. That was reflected in its advertising as Christmas 1936 approached:

Just Another Week Until Christmas

---

[163] LCL meant "Less than Car Load" and meant that the preferential rate for a full rail car did not apply.

We are showing the largest stock of merchandise for years. Make your selection and have it put away for delivery Christmas Eve Special Delivery from 8:00 to 11:00 p.m. We pack carefully all parcels for shipment by mail and express. Make your selection, we do the rest.[164]

1303 Third Avenue at Quebec Street (as of the fall of 1937)

The official opening at this location was held October 30, 1937. Configuration was spacious, featuring a 30 foot by 110 foot main floor with a mezzanine and a full basement. An unusual feature for a hardware store was inclusion of a ladies' lounge – a restroom fitted out with easy chairs and brocade drapes. The main floor was equipped with display tables for every type of hardware and building supplies, large appliances, bicycles, and sporting goods. Customers found small electrical appliances and radios on the mezzanine level. The basement housed a modern steam-heating system for the building and provided storage.

Norm Radley was hired as store manager with Harold Moffat and Frank Milburn working in sales.

The 1930s had been lean economic times. Full-time employment started to return around the end of the decade and the biggest boost came when 5,000 soldiers got stationed here in

---

[164] Advertisement published 17 December 1936, Prince George Citizen, p. 5.

1939. That helped stimulate the economy and The Northern became a major supplier to the Army. Around that time, Pinchie mines opened to get mercury for the war effort.

A.B. Moffat's approach to retail operating was to conduct business with a sales contract and a credit component. The contract entered into with customers allowed them to make monthly payments for a year. "The bankers told dad he would go broke when he operated on a 90-day free credit basis," remembers Harold. "But, through the years, more people came back to say how they appreciated the credit when they first came to Prince George. For many families and small businesses, it made all the difference."

Other stores commonly offered a deal of $100 off on buying a new washing machine. This was avoided for years by A.B. Moffat who thought it was degrading to his concept of honest business. But the pressure was on to imitate the deal.

Harold overheard an incident where Spike Enemark owed on his account with The Northern, and paid it all off. Then, his wife wanted a new stove, so he came and asked, "Alex, how much for cash?" It didn't work. He paid the going price!

Mechanical repairs to washers were done by Harold's brother, Earl. Second hand ones were brought in as trade-ins on new machines, and then the store sold those used ones as well.

Some customers travelled back out of Prince George on the local freight train that shunted the cars to and from towns to the south and McBride to the north.

Harold recalls standing at the corner of Third and Quebec and seeing the Army march by. People could watch the soldiers through the store windows. In the 1930s, the store stayed open Saturday nights until the last customer left. People came from out of town, and the Moffat family believed it was proper to oblige them by keeping the store open as late as necessary. The Northern was a major supplier in those years. Another outlet in town was run by Billy Blair. He carried mainly work clothes, saws, and some hardware.

The 1940s

The store's exterior at Third and Brunswick got a facelift in April 1941. Frank Moffatt[165] took on the job and ensured that the prominent location and its upstairs apartments got a new coat of stucco.

In addition to the responsibilities of business, Harold began taking on an even more active leadership role in the community. Perhaps inspired by his father's example of public service. A.B. Moffat had served as an Alderman from 1926 to 1929 and again from

---

[165] Frank Moffatt was a local contractor with a similar name, but not a relative.

1940 to 1943; was actively involved in the Chamber of Commerce; and elected President of the Prince George Rotary Club for 1944-45. Harold also invested his energy and attention in community groups.

The first Ratepayers' association in Prince George formed in November 1943 and elected Harold as its President. The group's purpose was to present concerns in a constructive manner to the city's administration.

When the veterans returned after the war in 1945, Prince George began returning to normal and the economy started to grow again.

There was one memorable and formative incident involving banking. Harold heard his father answer the telephone one day and the banker asked him when the overdraft would be covered. A credit of $25,000 to $30,000 had been arranged to purchase stock for the furniture salon after that store section was added. Harold knew that his father had paid for the expansion out of his own funds, and then had looked to bank funding for stock purposes. After overhearing that conversation, he suggested to his father that they should get another banker!

From the beginning, the emphasis was on the customer. Harold watched his dad wait on customers during the day, and then the expectation was to go home for dinner, but later would come back to the store.

At one point, the fertilizer business was added on. This was business that The Northern took over from Buckerfields. Fertilizer was obtained in bulk, pre-mixed, and weighed 80 pounds a sack. It had to be hand bagged in the warehouse.

This was an era when labour wasn't counted. One did what was necessary, and opened for business to suit the needs of customers. The store opened regularly at 8:00 a.m., with the sidewalk swept, and closed at 6:00 p.m. Everyone worked a fifty hour week over the five days a week the store was opened. Subsequent to that time, the store closed all day Mondays and was opened on Saturdays instead.

Harold got to do every job in the store. As a family member working for the store, that was expected. It was Harold's experience that that meant especially the ones nobody else wanted to do – like sweeping and cleaning.

A job he was especially good at was making tack and fitting it to the horses. There was a harness maker in town, Sibley, and The Northern also became a tack seller. The biggest part was assembling the harnesses. Most customers just bought the tack and then fit their own horses. There was an American farmer who bought tack – on the condition that Harold would come out to the farm and install it.

Later, The Northern got into the machinery business. The McLennan, McFeely & Prior chain was then operating in town as the other equipment supplier.

Harold's dad sold John Deere implements – harrows, discs, plows – all of them meant to be horse-drawn. The Northern also had the Case Agency (a desirable brand). Combines were coming into more common use. A warehouse was built on the CNR tracks, allowing winter activity for store employees in assembling combines. It was very cold in that warehouse over the winter months. Mainly the employees were cold because the clothing was inadequate, because it wasn't practical to heat a space that large. Among the main crops was excellent clover and timothy seed. Buckerfields came in and bought those crops.

Seeds and fertilizer were big sellers through the store in the war years. The advertising fit in with the idea of growing a victory garden, as in this example from the spring of 1940:

The war is on – SEEDS

During war time there is a greater necessity for putting in a larger garden, and wise gardeners will get their seeds early while choice is fair. We have a most complete stock of Bulk and Package Seeds, and can assure you our Prices are Better than seed or mail-order lists.

Don't overlook FERTILIZER for a larger yield. We carry BURNS PRESTO – which is second to none.[166]

As families could afford it, the modern push in the mid-1940s was to upgrade to electric kitchen ranges and refrigerators. The Northern carried the Frigidaire line – and those who wanted to have those appliances right away could apply for credit. The store's ads invited "Terms may be arranged according to W.P.T.B. Regulations."[167]

Third Avenue & Brunswick Location as of the spring of 1940

At first, The Northern occupied only part of the building. The upstairs was rented as apartments, and the downstairs space was rented to the post office and a customs office was set up in behind.

The first elevator was built by Keith Yorston, President of QM Machine Works. It was of simple construction – basically just a platform with a motor and basic plywood doors. It functioned very well, and was in operation until an elevator inspector turned up and insisted that it be replaced. After that, a new elevator was ordered from the Montgomery Elevator Company. It wasn't nearly as good, and had a smaller platform. But, it complied with the required code standards.

---

[166] Advertisement published 21 March 1940, Prince George Citizen, p. 9.

[167] Advertisement published 21 March 1946, Prince George Citizen, p. 7. The acronym is for "Wartime Prices Trade Board."

The Third and Brunswick location opened
for business on May 9, 1940 and for several
years, The Northern operated from both Third
Avenue locations.   During that decade, the
store's major hardware supplier was the
Marshall Wells company.

Within the first five years, Harold witnessed
some dramatic changes.   Renovations were
arranged to be done while his father went away
on holidays. Upstairs, partitions were torn out
from the apartments to convert the upper floor
to store use.   All the doors, plumbing and
salvageable material was sold – nothing was
wasted.

The entire area became devoted to furniture
display.   In   the   downstairs   area,   the
merchandise expanded into more appliances
and giftware in the space where the furniture
and post office had been located. Some stock
arrived from orders placed by A.B. Moffat after
his visits to the wholesale houses in Vancouver.
Other   stock   came   from   the   travellers   (as
salesmen were called in those days) who came
through the towns carrying samples and product
knowledge to line up orders for their companies.

The upstairs office was created and used to
conduct the business of the store as well as to
play   cards,   usually   every   Thursday   and
Saturday.   A particular favourite was a game
called Solo, which originated in Germany and
had been popular on this continent during the
Klondike gold rush.   Four men played it.   Two
played to begin with and the other two men

would then play against the winner of the first round. As for politics, only the activities of the Conservative party were ever allowed to be discussed in that room!

New plate glass windows – large for that era being 30 feet by 10 feet were installed at the ground floor facing Third Avenue and also on the side facing Brunswick Street.

The floor space for display expanded by an additional 1,800 square feet over the size of the original furniture showroom. That space allowed for introduction of Oriental rugs and linoleum floor covering. A.B. Moffat was particularly fond of carpets, and he liked to drape carpets along the interior walls. Bedroom, living room and dining room furniture occupied the centre floor. The central stairway led downstairs to the Bargain Basement.

During the early 1940s, Carl Johnson rigged up a wood-splitting machine. Crafted out of a big wagon wheel and the gas engine from an old power washer, it made for efficient work. Harold and two friends cut ten cords of wood in a day – sawing it into 16-inch lengths. It was customarily lent out to people for their personal use. As to its fate, in Harold's memory "It ended up at somebody's place. It should have been hauled to the museum. Bill Blackburn had a picture of it."

In 1945, Hilliard Clare began working for The Northern after school and on weekends. He stocked shelves and rode the delivery truck as a helper. Graduating from high school in 1947, that fall Thompson Ogg, the store's Secretary-Treasurer asked Hilliard to come to work in the office. His first day of full-time employment was January 15, 1948. That began a career which stretched through the next six decades, making him the store's longest serving employee. He recalls that in those early years the accounts were all hand-written and they had stand-up desks to do the ledger work – vastly different from the computerized systems the store had in 2005. Harold Moffat, as the founder's son, began working part-time as a child of twelve in 1927, took on full-time employment in 1933, and never retired.

The Quesnel store operated until A.B. Moffat's partner, Frank Whitmore, wanted out after 27 years because of plans to move to a warmer climate in California. A.B. Moffat sold that store on January 24, 1946 to Lloyd D. Harper & W.C. Willis. The Quesnel store continued to operate as The Willis-Harper Hardware & Furniture Co.

A.B. Moffat paid Frank out a few months later on April 8th. At that time, he had Harold become a shareholder. By October 1, 1946, Harold was appointed a director of the company. Ownership of the store was then shared amongst A.B. Moffat, Harold Moffat, and the company's secretary-treasurer, Thompson Ogg. Ogg's background had been in the lumber brokerage business which collapsed during the war. At that point, Ogg took up bookkeeping, a natural choice hearkening back to his previous experience as a bank manager.

Radio broadcasts were featured at 11:45 a.m. on Mondays, Wednesdays and Fridays broadcast on radio station CKPG. Leading in to the mid-day news, the topics kept pace with the seasons featuring household and farm advice and new stock arrivals at the store.

In 1947, a large addition to the premises at the corner of Third Avenue and Brunswick of 40 feet by 110 feet was designed by Vancouver architects Semmens and Watson. Construction by J.N. Dezell and Son was underway by March of 1948. The plans incorporated a full basement and second storey with a freight elevator and a private cafeteria for staff. Ultimately, the elevator shaft was included, awaiting installation of the elevator at some future date. Plans for the cafeteria were eliminated. There were two ramps – one running down to the basement where Earl Moffat oversaw appliance repair and another running up to the receiving bay. The building was heated by steam, circulated by electric fan units on each floor. Windows incorporated along forty feet of the top floor allowed merchandise to be seen from outside.

It took a week to move all the stock down Third Avenue from the corner of Quebec Street to the corner of Brunswick Street. Consolidation of the two locations happened the last week of July in 1948.

Another wood-splitting contraption was built in July of 1948 by Harold Moffat and J.E. Van Somer of 2454 Baillie in the Crescents district. The inspiration for the project came after seeing a similar machine being operated at McBride. Capable of splitting a cord of wood in an hour, the mechanical device made swinging an axe a thing of the dangerous wood-chopping past. Van Somer used it at his home and explained its operation as "a large wheel to the rim of which is affixed a heavy steel wedge. A two-stroke miniature gas engine supplies the motive power. With each revolution of the wheel, the steel wedge strikes the log hard against it and in the twinkling of an eye splits the wood in four pieces."[168]

In 1949, all the Moffat sons (Donn, Earl, Gilbert (Corky), John and Keith) were brought into the business. A few months later, long-time employee, Hilliard Clare, also became a shareholder and business partner.

The 1950s

The year 1951 saw A.B. Moffat make a business move which, in retrospect, was extremely progressive for the time. He brought his daughters, Betty, Alice and Joyce in to the business as equal partners.

With the closing of the Army camp after the Second World War, recovery of a peacetime economy began. Not that many young people

---

[168] Article published 15 July 1948, The Prince George Citizen, p. 10.

went away with the Army. Construction people stayed and there was an increase in population with returning soldiers.

The hardware business was slower to recover, due to a government policy that took all the profits but about $5,000 for each store. Harold's father figured he should have been allowed to keep $5,000 for each of the Furniture and the Hardware enterprises. He considered that they were separate businesses and the accounting for them had always been independent. The major wholesale suppliers were J.H. Ashdown, based in Edmonton and MacLelland & MacFealy (Mac & Mac), based in Vancouver but operating a warehouse in Prince George.

Returning veterans caused the bulge in business. Sawmills started and became the employment base for the city. There was some housing construction, but many of the Army buildings were moved into town. Some even became school dormitories. Homes were built in Millar Addition, Burden Street, Carney Street using salvaged lumber from Army buildings. Lumber produced by local sawmills was all meant to be exported.

There was a particularly special store fixture acquired during the mid 1950s. That was the purchase of the much-loved children's ride – a noble mechanical horse named Champion. A.B. Moffat purchased the ride from Isabel Electric, and for years, that company serviced it. He struck a deal that saw him trade a 16' aluminum boat with a 40 horsepower motor and a trailer for it. That ride was constructed before the era of "built-in-obsolescence" and was a device made to last. The sturdy motor needs very little repair or maintenance. Children of all ages still delight in riding Champion. Even a half century later, men who were the little boys of the Fifties return and bring their dimes to let their own children ride or even to re-live the experience themselves. The ride still costs ten cents, just as it has always done. The horse has paid for itself a hundred times over through the years.

A momentous event occurred in 1955. That was the year that company founder, A.B. Moffat, elected to retire. He had a different take on what that meant, because he came in every day, even for just a few hours, as long as his health permitted. Then, as during his entire working life, he always maintained a formal approach in his haberdashery. He never came in to work at the store without wearing a tie.[169]

---

[169] Conversation with Harold Moffat, 22 January 1998.

KELLY CUP WIN 1958

The Northern was always looking to modernize. One of the first paved parking lots was that at the rear of the store – paved with asphalt in 1957.

The 1960s

Harold's son, Ted, began working full time in the store's office in 1960.

In 1964, the store got a fairly extensive remodelling. Business was strong with the influx of new residents as the pulp mills were being built and new employees arrived with their families. Some of the floors got new linoleum tile. All new display fixtures were purchased – like the big gondolas in the main floor display areas. The overall re-design was handled by store planners Dixon & Murray.

Upstairs, the furniture department faced the challenge of strong sun streaming in through the bank of windows facing Third Avenue. The windows were covered over to cope with the need to keep furniture on display from fading and also to provide additional wall display space.

The old stairs to the second floor were replaced with a wider central stairway. Its wooden rails and spindles have been kept oiled and polished through the decades.

Expansion of the store's footprint was accomplished in 1965 with purchase of the adjacent building owned by the Zogas family. They rented it to the operators of a Five & Dime store. The two buildings had been constructed abutting each other, so it was a matter of opening up access inside. The biggest challenge, which went on for decades, was finding a successful weather membrane to stop rain leaking in from the joined rooftops overhead.

The 1970s

Harold Moffat was elected Mayor in the December 1969 election. He settled in to the Mayor's chair in early January 1970, taking the oath of office on January 5th. In that era, the role was considered a part-time job, so he was able to divide his time between managing the family business and overseeing the business of running the City of Prince George.[170]

A business decision was made in 1972 to align with Link Hardware – an Edmonton-based company which concentrated on wholesale hardware distribution throughout Western Canada. This was The Northern's first corporate affiliation. The decision to join with a major chain was made once it became apparent that a small hardware needed to benefit from greater buying power.

It was also 1972 that the store installed its first computer system. It was a Burroughs accounting software which was run on the punch card technology of the day. It kept track of general ledger information—payables; receivables. Ted Moffat attended a six week course in San Franciso on managing the system, which was part of the purchasing agreement. For as long as it was available, the store has had an automated accounting system.

The problem was to find a point-of-sale system which worked for the range of items needed to be accounted for in inventory. For decades, until that capability became available, inventory control was handled by the partners, each taking responsibility for an area of the store.

---

[170] The Mayor's job became funded as a full-time position in 1991, half way through the term John Backhouse was Mayor (1986 to 1996).

OLD GAS PUMP

For many years, The Northern was the regular advertising sponsor for the 8 o'clock morning news broadcast on CKPG. The station wanted to offer that high profile slot to Sears, which was the anchor tenant attracted into the Pine Centre Mall. With the mall's official opening on November 6, 1974 there was a new sponsor for the news after the station replaced

The Northern's advertisements with advertising from Sears.

The growing AMCO/Marshall Wells business required warehouse space. A suitable location became available – nearby on First Avenue and Queensway. That was a building which had been owned by businessman Ben Ginter and when his fortunes unravelled, the property was offered through a tax sale. It was purchased in 1978 and converted to warehouse use by adding a truck delivery bay.

During the 1970s, the practice of downtown stores closing on Wednesdays at 1:00 p.m. stopped. Instead, stores switched to closing all day on Mondays so staff could have two consecutive days off.

The 1980s

The decade of the 1980s was a period of economic downturn in British Columbia – particularly in the major industries of forestry and mining. However, The Northern experienced good business and had steady sales growth. No renovations to the store were undertaken in those years.

Another factor which affected retail sales was the high cost of borrowing. Interest rates reached a dizzying 21%. The Northern survived by realizing the staff had to pull together as a team. The various areas watched store purchasing carefully and inventory was kept to basic needs. The other factor was the loyal customer base. Despite other purchasing options, people kept returning and the trust level in the advice given was high.

Appliances could be traded in at The Northern and a credit applied against the purchase of the new one. Any repairs needed were done within the store and the trade-ins got sold as used appliances. Earl Moffat did most of the maintenance and repair work on used appliances.

The 1990s

TED MOFFAT

The family business is under the stewardship of Harold's son, Ted Moffat, who became President February 1, 1993. With his two cousins – Blair Moffat and Ian Moffat, they bought out the five brothers of the previous generation – Keith, Donn, the estate of Earl, John and Gilbert (Corky) and the shares of sisters Joyce, Betty and Alice in 1993. The Moffat Family Trust was established then (for all of Harold's grandchildren) as the fourth owner. The current ownership structure remains based within the family.

With retirement of the previous generation, along with them went their collective expertise in inventory control That needed to be replaced with a system which could produce fractional stock keeping units (SKUs). Keeping track of cumulative sales was believed the most desirable feature of inventory software. Ted started checking out available systems and chose the one developed by ProfitMaster Canada, headquartered in Winnipeg. Theirs had the best point-of-sale for the stock, and the software has since been adjusted and adapted. The Northern has served as a beta-test site for ProfitMaster's systems. As a further complication, there were three locations that needed to be folded in: the store, the warehouse and appliance centre, and the Amco outlet.[171]

The Link Hardware group was purchased by Home Hardware Stores Limited on December 31, 1980. The advantage for The Northern in keeping an alliance is the economies of scale realized with buying power of about a thousand stores. That purchasing capability helps keep prices competitive.

The warehouse, located on First Avenue at Victoria, underwent alterations and the downstairs floor of the store at Third and Brunswick was refixtured with new gondolas and other display equipment.

In 1994, the familiar old clock which sat atop the canopy for decades was taken down. It had become harder and harder to keep it running with accurate time. Its neon tubes were shot, and frequently the clock operated only on one side. That used to generate lots of calls from people working in the ScotiaBank building at Fourth Avenue and Victoria who would call the store to report that the clock wasn't running.

Hilliard Clare was sorry to see the end of the clock. "I was disappointed to see it go. It

---

[171] AMCO, was created as the Northern Hardware's wholesale division after the company purchased the assets of Marshall Wells. AMCO, a subsidiary of The Northern Hardware, was a name chosen by Ted Moffat as a tribute to his Grandfather. It represents "Alex Moffat Company."

had been a landmark for quite a while. But, every time it was wrong, we heard about it!"[172]

There was another reason that the clock had to go. Ted understood that although the Northern had been affiliated with the Home Hardware chain since 1972 some customers were unaware of that. He thought it was time to put up more prominent Home Hardware signage. The decision was made and the clock was taken down. Perhaps that gesture respected A.B. Moffat's adage, "Don't be a clock watcher." A large Home Hardware sign was put up in its place.

Changes in 1996 were more subtle. The store got newer, smaller windows and a Sensormatic security system was installed.

By January of 1997, it was time to consider replacement of the boiler in the main store. It was ordered and installation was completed by the end of June.

Another of the exterior changes happened in 1997 when Ted contracted with architect Trelle Morrow to redesign the store's front entrance. The ramp up to the door was levelled and the extra set of double doors got removed. The front windows were moved forward to create more window display area. A new, modern entry door and security system replaced the old one. By that year, the number of employees was 51 at the main store and another five at the warehouse. Fully stocked, the store's inventory

---

[172] Interview with Hilliard Clare, 9 August 2005.

represents an impressive array of equipment and household items.

Early on, Ted decided to turn around Harold's aversion to advertising. Up to that point, advertisements had been haphazard and planned only with a "by the seat of the pants" approach. At that point the ads were thought up in-house and placed to co-ordinate with the 52 flyers Home Hardware puts out each year. Ironically, there were costs associated with that scale of business – more employee time working with customers and doing deliveries plus the expenses which come associated with more volume. The Northern Hardware regularly places advertising to complement the Home Hardware flyers. Customers have come to count on the Northern to find products there which have been carried for decades as well as unique merchandise obtained through other suppliers.

For a five year period between 1995 and 1999, sales dropped by 35% due to the large population shift as people left the city to seek employment, primarily in Alberta. Another factor was the overall sense of uncertainty in the economy which caused customers to hold back on consumer spending. High rates of sales tax, compared with other jurisdictions, didn't help, either.

Despite the slowing of customer traffic through the store, Harold never departed from his dedication to giving people good, practical advice. A classic situation occurred one day in September 1998 when a customer was admiring a gleaming white Victorian-style range. Manufactured by the Elmira Stove Works, it was called "Cook's Delight" and had the antique look of yesteryear combined with the modern convenience of four gas burners and a sidecar attached with two electric burners. It was a grand appliance, worth every dollar of the more than $3,000 it would take to purchase. The eager customer had the brochure in her hands. Customers watched as Harold approached, motioning to the papers and asking "What do you have there?" She started expressing enthusiasm for the expectation of owning that range. Harold's responded, "You don't need that. All you need to cook on is a hotplate!"

Similar "rethink that purchase" advice happened in other areas. Harold told a woman about to purchase a $40.00 thermometer with a temperature probe to give both indoor and outdoor readings that it was a bad idea. "Knowing how cold it is outside will just keep you from doing things," but she bought it anyway. Another example happened at the fishing supplies counter. Once Harold realized the man purchasing a high-end rod had never gone fishing before, he talked him out of getting such a good one. "You don't need that expensive rod. Start with this one instead. If you like fishing and get good at it, you can come back to get that one." It can honestly be said that customers at The Northern are never pressured into purchases. The opposite is more likely to happen! On the surface, that might look like counterproductive retail strategy, but it's the reason why customers trust the Northern and value the advice given throughout the store.

As anyone might expect in a family business, Harold didn't take to much of the change he saw happening with what had been his store for so many decades. Rather than be confrontational, the staff started to organize any changes like installing new displays or equipment on Fridays because that was Harold's day off. Friday became known as "moving day" as the scramble would start to get something new in place before Harold was back on duty on Saturday morning!

Harold didn't keep his disapproval to himself. Ted heard him announce to a customer who came in to the store up the back stairs one day, "I hope you brought your map. That's the only way you're going to find anything!"

Despite his resistance to change and plummeting sales around 1998, it was Harold who recommended to son Ted that the store needed to invest in a computerized inventory system. The one chosen was from ProfitMaster Canada, sold by John Hamm who came out from Winnipeg to configure the system. The very latest in computerized cash registers were installed in 1998. They track thousands of items and track sales in such detail that it is possible to calculate the profit generated for every square foot of the store. Harold wants nothing to do with those machines and doesn't operate them himself. He gets a staff member to ring up sales.

Harold wasn't the only one who had reservations about the new cash registers. Hilliard Clare has worked with all the accounting systems used at the store, practically as far back as using a quill pen! He had some skepticism, too, about the switch. "At first I thought they were a real hazard, but they turned out to be a boon. We have better control over cash flow. They do inventory and tracking as well."[173] In prior years, inventory had been done the way it had always been done – with a "yeller" (presumably the one up on the ladder) and a "writer" (the one recording the quantity of items) and a code invented to convey what the wholesale price was for each item. Ten letters would get chosen to represent 0 to 9 – and with that, the cost to the store of every item could be known.

Like he's always done, Harold works at giving advice and telling customers where to look for the items they're seeking. The back counter at The Northern is where his friends know to find him. That is also the place where significant events are discussed and advice freely given. It is a fair statement that some of the most interesting conversations anyone could ever happen upon occur around that back counter.

The Northern Hardware has survived on customer loyalty, and through the decades, has supported the community making contributions to good causes and sports teams and remained

---

[173] Interview with Hilliard Clare, 9 August 2005.

loyal to its suppliers and supporting services. One example is that the company started out doing its banking with the Bank of Montreal. It still has the original account number, 5. To accommodate modern computer systems, it's now expressed on the bank records as 000 000 005.

Into the Millennium – 2000 and Beyond

The Coffee Gang, one of Prince George's most enduring institutions since the late 1930s, still meets daily from Monday to Saturday at 10:00 a.m. sharp. Once a powerful political group whose members virtually "ran" the city, it is still constituted with a membership of successful businessmen and community leaders. Harold Moffat and Hilliard Clare get there for 10:30 because they are both working and can't take as much time to talk as those who are already retired. No one is ever invited to join. Those who show up know by some form of osmosis that they belong. Local broadcaster Bob Harkins once said "You know you're a member when Hilliard Clare asks you for $30."[174]

The Coffee Club never developed any fanfare or rituals, but the group has a quirky tradition which all agree to uphold and respect. That is the recycling of a plastic floral arrangement which is used to cut down on the

---

[174] Comment by Bob Harkins interviewed by Valerie Giles 30 January 1997. By 2005, membership is up to $50 and the numbers have decreased from 22 to about a dozen.

costs of any tributes which might otherwise be required if any member becomes ill or is hospitalized. It's been around for decades and now is very old and bedraggled-looking – a few pastel flower spikes stuffed into a utilitarian-looking white bud vase which still has the original price sticker affixed. It gets passed around, and even distance is no deterrent to its delivery.

One example was the occasion when Bob Harkins was awaiting heart bypass surgery at St. Paul's Hospital in Vancouver. Sure enough, Hilliard Clare walked in to Bob's room carrying the arrangement which looked like it had been passed through some sawmill equipment. With him was a contraption assembled and sent by Harold Moffat. It was a board with plastic tubing tacked in place on it and instructions for the surgeon about the various sizes available to use in the operation. There was, of course, expectation that the tubes selected would be purchased from The Northern Hardware!

Inevitable change kept happening to the store locations. Renovations to the warehouse in March 2001 saw installation of new windows. By July, the air conditioning system needed attention, and the compressors on that system were all replaced. The next year in March, the major expense was upgrading the store's computer to incorporate the latest technology in servers.

The year 2005 has proven to be up there among the most expensive for upgrades. A new roof was installed over half the store in February.   Dramatic upgrades to the store's interior came in March and April when flooring on both levels was replaced.   Upstairs, the furniture department got light oak flooring throughout – a major job moving all the stock. The office area got new blue carpeting. Downstairs, carpeting covered up the red, green, black and yellow tiles which customers had trod for decades.   That investment signalled a solid commitment to the store's future.   The community felt assured that The Northern was here to stay.

In May, an upgrade was made to the security system, installing the capability to photograph activity in the store around the clock.

By July, the exterior got re-branded with red and white metal cladding – the corporate colours of Home Hardware.

The Northern Hardware has grown to become a comprehensive department store.   By 2005, its inventory reached more than 70,000 items.   Before the computerized inventory system was installed, it was necessary to keep larger volumes of stock on hand.   Now, items can be brought in when alerted by the system. The big Home Hardware truck arrives faithfully every Tuesday.

With that truck come items featured in the weekly flyer, and the stock familiar to the Home Hardware chain. Still in stock are items that the

Northern has always sold, but would not likely be found at any other store in the chain. Long-time customers know that old products like washboards and even chamber pots are sold there yet. All the tack needed for horses is there against the lower floor's back wall – and the expertise to fit it. Another traditional product at The Northern is the little red and white cardboard box of Iron Out "The All Purpose Rust and Stain Remover." It's still imported from Fort Wayne, Indianna, and always will be.

The store still lives up to its long-time motto "If we don't have it; you don't need it." Actually, Harold Moffat might tell you that even if it's in stock!

Chapter IX

Working Retirement

Harold Moffat turned 65 on September 24, 1980. To many others, that event might have signalled the time to retire. Not having any interest in the idea of retirement, he kept coming to work every day. The back counter at The Northern is where everybody knows to find him. It's an opportunity to get advice on almost any subject and a chance to hear some of the most interesting conversations anybody could ever hope to stumble across!

Up until the fall of 2004, Harold went out to his farm property near the airport every evening to tend to his much-loved horses. For years, he hitched them to sulkies and ran them on an oval track – training them for racing on tracks in the Lower Mainland and Alberta. In later years, the horses were hitched to a trailer behind his old red pickup truck and they'd make the laps that way – good weather and bad. Keeping those horses in shape was more than an obligation. It has always been obvious that Harold loved his animals.

The work of looking after them has repaid him by keeping him physically active during years when most people fall into a sedentary life. Feeding horses involves moving heavy bales of hay and the movement required to groom and hitch them to the training cart helped maintain flexibility and mobility in the keeper! For a long time, Harold was able to jog with the horses as he put them through their paces. Even after he started driving the oval, there was still the exercise in getting the horses hitched to their training cart to run behind. In addition to the evening visits, Harold spent his day off, Friday, at the barn with his horses.

Looking back over all the horses he's owned, there have been some favourites. At one time, he had sixty-five horses, but pared the stock down to 14 by 1998 and to just a few by 2000. Harold acknowledges that the one named "Overburden" was his best horse. He was the colt born in 1972 to Harold's racehorse, "Motherlode." In a 1998 interview, Harold told Prince George Citizen reporter Bernice Trick "Overburden became a success at the race track, holding the track record in Edmonton for a season, and being voted the horse of the year during the late 1970s."[175] After Overburden, Harold's next best racer was "Billy Barker." That horse often raced at the same time as Overburden. "Often, the two of them had first and second placings."[176] A favourite horse name was "Northern" and he estimates that he put that moniker as the first name on at least seventy horses over the years.

Despite putting in full days, Harold always had time for lively discussions (on political

---

[175] Article "Sport of kings? Heck no, it's the sport of dreamers," Prince George Citizen, 22 June 1998, p. 13.
[176] Ibid.

topics, especially) – and he cared to share his long experience and perspective with the politicians and decision-makers of the day. There were two favourite venues for transmitting his opinions. The first was directly by letter to an official's office and the second was through letters to the editor of the Prince George Citizen. The latter allowed more people to become aware of what he was thinking and to engage in the discussion by showing up at the store. Every time Harold Moffat put pen to paper, there was bound to be reaction. That is how he became the catalyst for an ever-expanding list of topics and community issues.

Harold focussed his attention during the summer of 1993 on the issue of garbage disposal. Addressing his suggestion to the Chairman of the Prince George Regional District of Fraser—Fort George, he made the suggestion that the district should consider incineration as the answer. His letter suggested "The only way to go is to burn everything – refrigerators, stoves, you name it. From this heat you can generate power." He cited research done by Kirk MacMillan, an engineer at Canfor, whose research produced a plan to use city garbage as a heat source for the pulp mills. He continued:

> It was my contention that BC Hydro should be the agency to develop such a project. There is valuable research material available due to the study of coal-burning thermal power at Hat Creek. Besides which the cost of power

can be meshed in with their other projects and they have the know-how in financing mega projects. It may be necessary to build a rail line from Ashcroft and Clinton to Hat Creek, which would be a logical site as they could use the coal for a supporting fuel.[177]

Receiving no promise of action on the issue from the Regional District, Harold attempted to engage the interest of reporters at The Citizen. That, and other issues, began weighing on him and he set out his concerns in point form in an open letter to the newspaper's publisher. He approached the newspaper and tried to arrange to purchase advertising space to ensure that it would be published. The newspaper refused.

As a fall-back plan, Harold arranged to have his letter printed as a handbill with the advertisement copy on one side and a letter of explanation on the other. This was the content:

Letter to the Publisher

February 1994

Mr. McNair, Publisher, Prince George Citizen

On September 15, 1993, I wrote you to enquire what has happened to the investigative reporter as your newspaper, at the most, has two pages

---

[177] Letter to Chairman, Prince George Regional District of Fraser—Fort George, 26 July 1993.

of local interest. No one has questioned
the following:

1. Who is responsible for the high costs
    and where is the money coming from
    for the access road to the University?
2. The relative costs of the proposed
    capital expenditures versus similar
    complexes in other cities.
3. The $50 million dollar waste disposal
    plan of the Regional District.
4. The Bank of Montreal on why they
    could not have built a complex at least
    comparable to Kamloops.
5. Why City Hall keeps pressing
    Cambridge on development plans when
    all the time they are entertaining
    proposals to develop on the old PGARA
    site?
6. The use of three-quarters of Third
    Avenue for a park when there was no
    opposition to it. Or whether the
    legalities were processed wherein one
    could protest or how much the
    downtown area received in
    compensation?
7. No one advised the public that the
    Community Plan pulled out hectares of
    land from the recreational area for
    commercial development.

Since writing the above, it was my
experience to participate and observe
what has happened at City Hall.
Firstly, you submit your proposal in
writing, you are then invited to an in

camera meeting where Council has already been briefed by Management on their reasons to oppose or endorse. One is then invited to the Council Chambers to make the public presentation. However, Council has been in an in camera meeting for three hours previous, so their public forum is nothing more than a puppet show. The two outgoing aldermen make the motion to endorse their position. We were then chastised for not being aware of the Community Plan meetings and that the valuable land in question was yielding minimal return. It was nice to find there were many thousand more that use the present site that were not aware of the proposal. It also made us wonder what are the returns from Carrie Jane Gray Park and Fort George Park.

It is past time that public business was put out on the table and the intrigue of management is divulged. The stealth by which the $36,000 publicity scheme on the Multiplex was launched with no mention of the (two million a year) operating cost. Why should there be two buildings opposite sites when the heat from one could heat the other and the same engineering crew could operate the joint plants and the same for management? Why do we have to go out of town for architects and engineers?

What did Pine Valley present at their in camera meeting? What are the machinations between the Golf Club, City and Pine Centre and the removal of soccer from Rotary Stadium? What goes on between the Realtor, the development manager and town planner and what other plans are under the table?

With every jurisdiction in Canada planning down spending, our Council allows management to use the cost of living index for an increase. They give themselves a salary increase which will reflect in all negotiations and be an excuse for the Regional District and School Board to also increase their salaries. Speaking of School Boards, who is going to divulge the ailments of Ron Brent built out of the best coast fir forty years after King George V and Central Fort George.

Mr. Publisher, I submit that you should examine the role of The Citizen to the Citizens.

H.A. Moffat

His message to the people of Prince George was:

29 March 1994

Letter to the Citizens of Prince George

Dear Citizen:

Attached for your information please find a copy of a paid ad (on reverse) that I submitted to the Prince George Citizen for publication. It was refused because they claimed the reference to non-investigative reporting and limited local news to be untrue.

On the date of refusal (February 10, 1994), there was only one page of local news, including the sports pages. You be the judge of investigative reporting. I am therefore using this method to circumvent the restrictions of freedom of speech.

You also never heard that I wrote to the regional boards of both Prince George and Quesnel, stating that they should consider the proposal that ALL garbage, wood waste and appliances from ALL of B.C. be rail-lined to Hat Creek and burnt in a thermal generating plant.

When I was mayor, Kirk MacMillan of Canfor designed such a plant to burn our garbage. However, concessions were made by the gas companies, therefore it was not viable. B.C. Hydro have complete plans in mothballs for a coal thermal plant, plus a coal deposit, the distribution system and financing ability and fully suited as a provincial authority to manage a provincial problem.

It would mean rail extensions from Clinton and Ashcroft, which is no problem. In fact, this should be done to allow alternate routing in case of a disaster in the southern area rail lines.

In any case, we should not be first to indulge in any extravagant venture, especially when we have at least 50 years of garbage burial grounds and when $50 million is only going to do a 50% job, if that.

Least of all, we should not be set up for a bureaucracy of teacher staffing, whereby another governmental department would be put in place to teach the general public how to package their garbage. I have advised the government that it is past time that a county system of government be established. The duplication of overhead at all levels is something the government must look at.

I have advised the chairmen of the Multiplex undertaking that they should study the advisability of establishing the two units in one cavern inside Cranbrook Hill, where they quarried the rock out to build the road to the pulp mills. Norway did this for US$18,500,000. They spent nearly one half again as much to go inside as compared to the outside, but the extra cost would be paid off in 15 years from the savings in operating and co-ordination of pool and arena. Such a plan would be a reason to hire local engineers and architects that have cost us a lot to educate.

It would appear that the lobbyists for the WHL franchise are putting pressure on the advisory committee to move without deliberation on cost cutting on the Multiplex or the Norwegian plan. If the Spruce Kings have all this advertising money to lobby, then perhaps they should be paying higher rental fees.

Respectfully submitted

H.A. Moffat[178]

Advice was offered to Premier Harcourt about the means to achieve fiscal responsibility in the provincial budget. Some excerpts:

28 February 1994

I suggest that you should take a leadership stand of no tax increases under any circumstances and there will be no borrowing except for essential services until we get the deficit under control.

and

---

[178] Handbill printed and circulated by Harold Moffat during March 1994.

Another area that I think you should examine is an appreciation property tax which would allow a low income earner to defer a high tax until the sale of property.

There was some expression of disappointment that the energy suggestion didn't get taken up:

Through our Regional District I understand that your environmental authorities rejected my plan to them that all the garbage, wood waste, appliances etc. of B.C. be moved via our railways to Hat Creek and that BC Hydro de-moth ball the plans for the coal thermal plant.

The letter ranged over a number of other topics, and then ended with the friendly closing:

Sorry to be so long winded but felt I must make you aware of some of the avenues I feel you can use to enhance your government and our province.

Yours truly,

H.A. Moffat[179]

Realizing that he was not finding any favourable response from the New Democrat government, the next year Harold offered his ideas to Jack Weisgerber, then leader of the Reform Party in British Columbia. The intent

---

[179] Letter to Premier Mike Harcourt, 28 February 1994.

was to offer some suggestions which might be incorporated into that party's policy platform.

He advocated that the system of provincial boards be eliminated now that they were populated by people who "all vote themselves salaries" instead of being volunteers as they were in the past. Another suggestion was that consideration be given to establishment of county governments to oversee civic management, school boards, hospitals, highways, and policing in local areas.

The one area singled out for provincial management was the environment. There followed the garbage disposal idea to be managed by BC Hydro, suggesting the construction of a thermal plant at Hat Creek to burn all the garbage in the province. Handwritten after his signature, Harold challenged Jack Weisgerber to act saying "P.S. Have never had a reply so will leave it up to you to at least prod someone to invoke the garbage disposal proposal."[180]

There were some ideas shared with Glen Clark during the time he served as Premier. Harold offered them qualifying his experience as a former school trustee, mayor, Regional District representative and director of the B.C. Power Corporation saying "I would like to pass on to you these observations. I am sure that implementation would cut costs at all levels."[181]

---

[180] Letter to Jack Weisgerber, Leader, BC Reform Party, 9 May 1995.
[181] Letter to the Hon. Glen Clark, Premier 9 July 1996.

Included in the range of topics was concern about the waste of having schools shut down for such long periods ever year:

> Another area you should investigate is the school system. In this enlightened world, we are still operating our schools as they did when Johnny had to stay home to bring in the crops. Our classrooms are used not more than 190 days a year. Besides lengthening out the school year, double shifting should be invoked.[182]

Premier Clark also got alerted about the garbage issue:

> One of the most important problems facing every municipality and district is garbage disposal. In our area, the projection is $50 million to meet the decree of your Government. In our case, we have a natural ravine that would do 100 years.
>
> I proposed to both the Regional Districts and the Mayors of the North, that they pressure the Government to have BC Hydro build the coal thermal unit that they have the plans in mothballs at Hat Creek. That the total cost of a rail connection from Ashcroft and Clinton, both railways and the BC Rail be included.

---

[182] Ibid.

The railways, in lieu of taxes, would transport the garbage. The Island would have to use the rail barge. The coal would be conserved, power would be generated and an ever-mounting problem would be solved. Besides, a gravel-like substance ideal for roads and roofing would result as a by-product.

Sorry to be so long winded. W.A.C. Bennett used to tell me that if I couldn't get it on one page, don't write him. It meant more letters.

Respectfully submitted,

H.A. Moffat[183]

In 1996, Premier Clark appointed the Hon. Dan Miller as Deputy Premier. It occurred to Harold that there should be some continuity of communication, so a free-wheeling letter was sent off to him near the end of that year. It reads like an animated conversation:

Hon. Dan Miller

Dear Sir:

Some time ago I wrote your Premier (a copy enclosed) with some suggestions to save money and to make use in a more lasting way of other mounting costs re: garbage disposal. He replied saying he was forwarding the suggestions to the

---

[183] Ibid.

various departments. To date, I have seen no mention but realize he is a busy man. He would be a lot less busy if he were firing the questions instead of answering.

You keep the media confused by coming up with questions; you want answers. Such as – the idea to purchase the C.N.R. from Jasper to Prince Rupert or at least from Prince George so we would be in a position to set rates that would increase the use of the ports in the west. When that dies down, you propose that we look at purchasing the line from Edmonton to Dawson Creek.

With the flooding of the Nechako, maybe you should re-examine the stop work order on Alcan's tunnel. What's going to happen when the Fraser floods out the Lower Mainland all because the environmentalists thwarted the dam on the McGregor?

As Minister of Municipalities[184], you can throw out the following. County form of government, a provincial garbage collection system to produce electricity. A formula for setting remuneration for municipal, regional district, and school board members. A longer school year,

---

[184] The Hon. Dan Miller served as Minister of Municipal Affairs from June 1996 to January 1997.

double shifting and the strap[185] in the classroom.

Another area you should examine is putting a freeze on the borrowing of funds by municipalities for non-essential facilities and only function at an operating loss paid for by an everlasting levy on the taxpayer. While you are at it, examine the Library policy. How come the users pay nothing for use?

Another thing that bothers me is that in this day and age of stress on moving product that we have two rail lines both going to and from through the canyon. Why there is not one way in and one way out is beyond me. Of course, the crews would not have time to sleep while they wait on a siding that would not have to be kept up.

All the best,

H.A. Moffat[186]

---

[185] This plea for the return of corporal punishment would not have sympathetic reception with any New Democratic Party government. The strap was removed from British Columbia schools by Education Minister Eileen Dailly. Symbolically, she chose Valentine's Day in 1973 to make that gesture. In a 1982 interview she reflected on that saying "I admit that this is something that I wanted to do, and I did it without much consultation. I wanted to set a tone in the schools, and it was my personal project to get violence out of the schools. The announcement was made on Valentine's Day…..I don't think that any government would put corporal punishment back."

[186] Handwritten letter to the Hon. Dan Miller, 2 December 1996.

Ideas for turning around the economy kept percolating. A selection of wide-ranging topics appeared in the local newspaper – separated out from the usual mix of letters to the editor – under the headline "Former mayor offers cure for the economy." The suggestions were meant to provoke debate and included the rather controversial suggestion that everybody on the government payroll, including pensioners, should be required to take a tax cut. In a highly-unionized population, that suggestion would have the buoyancy of a boat anchor.

That letter included the suggestion that the provincial sales tax should be eliminated to put this province on equal footing with Albertans – whose oil economy has provided well enough to that province's coffers that a sales tax isn't needed.

There were specific suggestions about the Alcan tunnel, handling bark beetle-killed wood, exporting electricity and water and garbage disposal. On the chance that any of these is eventually followed up, it's on the record that Harold thought up all of these ideas during the 1990s. He proposed:

> That we reactivate the Alcan tunnel. I have lived here 80 odd years and the Nechako, without the dam, fluctuated more than with the dam. The development at Kitimat has done more for Prince George than anything else. We need jobs, not wasting money on a scientific study of the river.

Make it a policy that if anyone can find a resource that will create product and jobs, in any area of our province, parks or others, there will be access with minimal regulation. Here, we are going to burn the bug-infested trees in Tweedsmuir Park instead of making a marketable product and employing more people. Eco-freaking is costing us our province.

We should negotiate contracts with provinces to our east and with the U.S. to deliver electricity that would make us a profit. The first should be the McGregor Dam. The water would go north to be generated through the turbines at the Bennett Dam. It would also relieve the problem of low water tables at Mackenzie and, above all, provide a control valve on the flooding of the Lower Mainland. With controls on the Nechako and McGregor, we should be able to effect less damage.

Promote the export of water to the States and bring dollars to our treasury. Taking water from the Revelstoke Dam should be no problem. We have the Stikine and Iskut watersheds to create untold power generation with no flooding of land and minimal damage to fisheries.

Build a garbage disposal power generating plant at Hat Creek where we have a coal resource. Plans for such a plant are complete and in moth balls at BC Hydro. It would mean a rail connection to Ashcroft to connect the main lines and BC Rail from Clinton. This station would burn everything. The railways would move the product in lieu of taxes. The rail cars from Vancouver Island could be barged to Squamish and from the Queen Charlotte Islands to Prince Rupert. We would eliminate the multi-millions spent on the burying program. $50 million is forecast for our region and we have holes that are there for another hundred years.[187]

Over the years, the Prince George Citizen has faithfully published letters from Harold Moffat...with the one exception when he chastised the reporters for coming up short on investigative capabilities and focus on local issues. The editors evidently looked forward to hearing from him and provided a platform for his views to be shared. An indication that his views were respected and shared came with the publication of letters from other readers. Two examples were:

Mr. Moffat has known this town from the days of wooden sidewalks...and he has knowledge and insight into what has taken place over the years. He has

---

[187] Excerpt from letter to the Editor, Prince George Citizen, published 27 November 1998, p. 5.

served the city well and had the confidence and faith of the people when they elected him mayor.

We all have our opinions about governments, about present-day shortcomings, about how the economy is affecting our citizens and, in many cases, jeopardizing their livelihoods. Harold Moffat put into words the thoughts of many.[188]

and

He is a hard-working citizen who has devoted time and effort in serving Prince George and has the well being and goodwill of the city in his heart.

He doesn't beat around the bush when expressing his opinions, and for this he is to be commended.[189]

Announcement of a proposed rate increase for natural gas customers caused concern in the spring of 2000. The BC Utilities Commission received some considered advice from Harold who made the point that there should be some rate relief to those areas of the province more dependent upon the natural gas resource:

Gas, a non-renewable resource, should be allocated according to some long-term inventory base.

---

[188] "H. Moffat writes thoughts of many," Letter from Olga Whellen, Vanderhoof, Prince George Citizen, 11 March 1999, p. 4.
[189] "Our former mayor tells it like it is…" Letter from James Stanhope, Prince George, Prince George Citizen, 12 March 1999, p. 4.

It is past time that rates for gas and hydro be set on a formula that relates to climatic extra use and the fact that the product originates in the north.

You should consider the impact this increase will have on the mills, the businesses and the wage earner – all of which are struggling with the past increases of gas, hydro and gasoline – and hurt more in the north than in the south.[190]

HAROLD MOFFAT AND THE CITY – BOTH 85 IN 2000

After Pat Bell was elected in May 2001 as MLA representing the riding of Prince George—North, some considered advice was coming his way, too. Harold began by stating he "would

---

[190] Letter to BC Utilities Commission, 13 June 2000.

offer the following thoughts on ways to turn the province around."[191]   One concept raised for consideration concerned development of power sources from which excess power could be sold to the United States:

> Namely, the third site on the Peace. Damming of the McGregor to produce power and add more water to Williston Lake, but above all to prevent a flood in the lower mainland that could be disastrous. [192]

The idea of burning all the province's garbage at Hat Creek was again flown, with the suggestion of linking railway routes to supply it.

There was environmental advice included:

> You should consult with Alcan to finish their tunnel to fulfill the need for power or an increase in production at Kitimat. In the meantime, stop the plan to spend a hundred million dollars on a cold water discharge at the Nechako dam. Some seventy years ago, we swam in the Nechako and it was really warm. The river was so low you could wade the river just south of the Cameron Street bridge. All the time, the salmon runs went on. It is the off-shore fisheries, nets along the rivers and predators, along with the Jet-boat activities that

---

[191] Excerpts from undated, handwritten letter addressed to Pat Bell, MLA
[192] Ibid.

have stressed the resource, not lack of water or temperature.[193]

Thinking about potential job creation, development of the mining sector was cited as a good possibility – as long as projects were entered into with a minimum 25-year life span.

> Would fly this kite—Expropriate the CN line from Jasper to Rupert. Instruct the BC Rail to set rates on grain from the Peace River that guarantee revitalizing of that part's grain business. With the China market a strong possibility for lumber and the Rupert port being closer than other ports, we should be able to sell it cheaper than others.

> Pat, the above are just some of the points that need to be addressed. We have to create jobs especially with the potential shut downs of our lumber sector. Am available at any time to expand on the ideas expressed and others on the mind.

> Yours truly,

> H.A. Moffat[194]

Writing directly to politicians – especially covering a range of topics in a letter – did not produce responses. In some cases, letters were merely ignored. Deciding it was time to get discussion of his pet projects provoked and out

---

[193] Ibid.
[194] Ibid.

there once again, Harold resorted to a paid advertisement in the newspaper. This time, the advertising department obliged by accepting the copy and even provided a bold headline. The newspaper was careful, though, to add the words "paid advertisement" over top of the eye-catching title of "Stupid, Stupid, Stupid!"

This was the text published:

Stupid that the dictatorship of the day, the provincial government, puts a ban on BC Hydro from further development of Hydro sources.

Would they tell us who and where can private developers produce power with a Renewable Resource cheaper than Site C.

We once had private power by the name of BC Electric. They were stymieing the growth of the province when W.A.C. Bennett expropriated it. From there we built the Peace and Columbia simultaneously. We built the PGE into BC Rail from Squamish to Vancouver and from Quesnel to Fort Nelson. To get the financing we must have shown a good return on the investment.

Stupid to let private parties produce power from non renewable resources.

When is this government going to wake up to the fact that one of these years the Fraser River will flood out billions of dollars of real estate in the south. Who can build the dam and power plant on the McGregor River cheaper than Hydro? Especially so when the stored water will flow north through the three generating stations. Three, that is, if site C is developed.

The fear of the northern fish entering the Fraser is a farce. Why are they not prevalent in Summit Lake?

Stupid to transfer any of the operations within Hydro to an outside source.

For those who analyzed the proposal surely they would find the ways to become more productive and efficient themselves.

Stupid to support the transformation to an outfit out of a free tax haven.

It is bad enough that we have the Irvings in the Maritimes and Paul Martin's shipping interest headquartered in Bermuda.

With Kyoto in controversy, it is past time that Canada took stock of all potential renewable power resources and that we set up a grid that will move power from the west to the east and vice versa in the east. Such a survey should look at the development of power from garbage and wood waste. Hydro has all the engineering completed on a coal generated power complex at Hat Creek. I suggest that this plant be built at Hat

Creek where there is coal as a back up but it be modified to burn all the garbage from the province. It would mean a rail connection from Clinton to Ashcroft. I am told by engineers that this would be no problem. Besides producing power, it would eliminate the enormous cost of burying and the subsequent problems with the decaying explosive gases. Vancouver Island could be accommodated through Squamish and the Queen Charlottes through Prince Rupert.

It is stupid to be trucking garbage out of Vancouver to Cache Creek. I understand they are looking at the Douglas Lake Ranch as a future destination. Just as stupid that we are trucking garbage from Valemount to be buried in a hole in Prince George. There is talk that it is going to cost $50 million to bury garbage in this Regional District.

Stupid to run a Power Smart Program when you are in the power business. The more that is used, the more you make.

Stupid to tell the people to plug their key holes in their door locks while the Building Inspector is forcing people to cut up to a 6" hole to the outside to give the furnace air.

We have the Iskut River that can handle many dams and generating stations. I think, seven, with minimal flooding. A true gem.

We then have the Stikine that has mammoth potential with no harm to fish stocks.

Both projects have engineering facts on record at BC Hydro.

We have the Alcan project that should be reexamined in view of the return of the fish population.

It is past time that the government spent more time creating job opportunities by building power projects. By opening up parks for any venture that will create jobs. The Tachanini has a very rich mineral venture. We know that there is a viable mineral project on the edge of Tweedsmuir Park providing they can build a road through the park. We have the environmentalists protecting against a mineral appraisal in the Chilcotin.

Stupid, Stupid, to preserve land for parks that could produce products that could feed people.

Stupid, to be selling our non-renewable natural gas to the controversial proposed power plant south of our border at a price that inflates the price we pay for gas.

At the same time the pollution drifts into our already over-polluted Fraser Valley. Surely we can come to a long term contract that guarantees a profit to both parties.

It is past time we reexamined the $1/2 million a year that we pay to the Yanks to not flood a few acres of non productive land on our borders.

Respectfully submitted,

Harold Moffat[195]

As soon as the provincial government announced the intention to sell BC Rail, Harold Moffat enjoined the debate, strongly opposing any notion of giving up such an important asset. He had the unique perspective of a lifetime's history in Prince George and an understanding of the importance of the railway to the regional economy.

The steel rails which connected Fort George to points east were laid across the Fraser River rail bridge and connected to track leading to the townsite on January 27, 1914. Twenty months later, Harold was born and he grew up understanding the importance of the railway to his birthplace.

As might be expected, he thought through the issue and had a suggestion which he posed in another letter to the editor:

---

[195] Advertisement published 11 January 2003.

Dear Sir:

I am most strenuously opposed to the transfer of BC Rail to the CNR, and will do everything and anything to upset the argument and those in favour of this disaster.

When BC Rail (then called Pacific Great Eastern) arrived in Prince George in 1954,[196] the CNR freight rates decreased by one-half.

There was an immediate transfer of business from Edmonton to Vancouver. When there is a monopoly there is no need to go north and give Fort St. John a rail terminal. Prior to that all the grain was trucked to Dawson Creek.

The push to Fort Nelson created industry in that area. As it did for Tumbler Ridge and increased business for the Port of Prince Rupert. Can you foresee the CN building a spur into Fort St. James when they could force them to use Vanderhoof as they did?

As chairman of the city's Industrial Development Commission in the '50s, I can tell you it would have been a monstrous job to locate the pulp mills

---

[196] A celebration was held to mark the connection of the PGE tracks between Prince George and Quesnel on November 1, 1952. The PGE's line connecting Squamish and Vancouver was completed in 1954. The first passenger train arrived in Prince George at 6:05 p.m. on Wednesday August 29, 1956.

north of the city. It was BC Rail that came up with a freight rate that made it possible to compete with other pulp mills on the waterfronts.

The extension of BC Rail north of Quesnel was the most important factor in the development of BC.

It was a sad day when they halted the extension of Dease Lake. We owe it to that sector of our province to open up its untold resources and to show the powers that be that we are on our way to Alaska.

BC Rail should remain as our catalyst for the development of our province and not as a pawn to pay off our debt and as a sweetener to the municipalities for short-term gains.

With proper management, BC Rail should produce a profit, something the Yankee-Doodle CN will develop at our expense.

But regardless, we subsidize the ferry systems, we subsidize the trucking system with the cost of the maintenance of our highways.

What should be done is, we expropriate the CNR line from Red Pass to Rupert and put it under BC Rail. In this way, we can set rates that would make Prince Rupert the port we have waited all these years to develop.

H.A. Moffat[197]

A fire levelled the Yellowhead Inn and the adjoining branch of the Bank of Montreal in August 2003. The bank's decision was to rebuild, and plans were drawn for an 11,000 square foot building to replace that branch at the corner of 15th Avenue and Central Street. The new building has room to consolidate the bank's branches, and that precipitated announcement that the Third Avenue location would be closed.

The first bank in South Fort George was the Bank of British North America which established in a tent in 1910. It later amalgamated with the Bank of Montreal, and that bank can claim to be the longest-serving financial institution in this region. A shack replaced the tent and after the city incorporated in 1915, that little building was placed on skids and dragged downtown. Eventually, a more permanent structure was built at the corner of Third Avenue and Quebec Street in 1920. After 85 years, people had gotten used to the idea that the Bank of Montreal was located on that corner.

Early in 2005, the bank was preparing its customers for the move from downtown to the newly-built banking centre named Citygate on Central Street. The bank announced early in

---

[197] "Let's improve BC Rail, not sell it," Prince George Citizen, 2 February 2004, p. 4.

February that the closing date for its venerable old location would be May 13, 2005.

The Northern Hardware & Furniture Company Ltd. had been one of the oldest clients. The store's account number ("5") had been assigned when A.B. Moffat and Frank Whitmore started their company in 1919. It was logical that the first person the newspaper would approach for comment would be Harold Moffat.

Harold's response was to declare the move "a total disaster to the redevelopment of the downtown core."[198] His belief that this was a mistake was so strong that he wanted City Council to intervene and establish a phone-in petition so customers upset with the move could register their feelings by indicating an unwillingness to move accounts to the new branch. "My name can head the list," he declared.[199]

Harold Alexander Moffat has forever respected the values with which he was raised. He's always been forthright in his opinions; true to his convictions; and loyal to his friends. Taught by his Father's example to care about this community, he embraced that same commitment to service. His legacy to the city for the decisions he made or guided while on school board, as mayor, and as a prominent businessman, is considerable. He and the Northern Hardware, the successful business he

---

[198] "Bank defends move to leave downtown," Prince George Citizen, 3 February 2005, p. 3.
[199] Ibid.

and his family built, are both inextricably bound to the identity and image of Prince George.

A GROUP PHOTO OF THE STAFF AT NORTHERN HARDWARE. 1948
© WALLY WEST COLLECTION AT THE EXPLORATION PLACE

AN EXTERIOR VIEW OF NORTHERN HARDWARE. 1948
© WALLY WEST COLLECTION AT THE EXPLORATION PLACE

A WINDOW DISPLAY AT NORTHERN HARDWARE IN 1961, PROMOTING THE
BOY SCOUTS. 1961
© WALLY WEST COLLECTION AT THE EXPLORATION PLACE

INSIDE NORTHERN HARDWARE AND FURNITURE, LOCATED AT 1386 THIRD
AVENUE. APRIL 1 1964
© WALLY WEST COLLECTION AT THE EXPLORATION PLACE

THE APLIANCE AREA AT NORTHERN HARDWARE. APRIL 1 1964
© WALLY WEST COLLECTION AT THE EXPLORATION PLACE

AN INTERIOR VIEW OF THE SPORTING GOODS PLUS THE LAWN AND GARDEN
AREAS AT NORTHERN HARDWARE. APRIL 1 1964
© WALLY WEST COLLECTION AT THE EXPLORATION PLACE

Index

Printed in the United States
82298LV00002B/184-417